*BELIEFS
THAT
MATTER*

BELIEFS THAT MATTER

by
GANSE LITTLE

Philadelphia
THE WESTMINSTER PRESS

Library of Congress Catalog Card No.: 57–9603

PRINTED IN THE UNITED STATES OF AMERICA

To My Father

CONTENTS

FOREWORD

THE chapters of this book were first preached as sermons in the winter and spring of 1951–1952 in the Broad Street Presbyterian Church of Columbus, Ohio, in a valiant attempt to put into one consecutive series the basic content of our Protestant Christian faith. My desire was so to interpret " orthodox " doctrine and " orthodox " language as to help make doctrine and language alike meaningful to a twentieth-century Christian congregation. (As it turned out, this series was my valedictory at the conclusion of twelve stirring and fruitful years, 1940–1952, before moving to Pasadena.) These same sermons were reworked and preached again before the congregation of the Pasadena Presbyterian Church in the winter and spring of 1956. Upon each occasion there were many requests from parishioners who professed to be helped by them, proposing that they be published in book form.

Then came the completely unsolicited invitation to serve as the summer substitute for Dr. Ralph Sockman on the National Radio Pulpit for the months of July, August, and September of 1956. My acceptance of that request was made possible in large part by the generous interest in the venture of our Board of Christian Education of the Presbyterian Church in the U.S.A. It seemed fitting and worth-while to use before this larger congregation what is, after all, a series

9

of " teaching sermons." (The interpretations given here are, of course, my own and do not necessarily reflect the approaches used by the Board of Christian Education in its teaching program.) The reaction of a nationwide audience included reiterated demands that I consider seriously the matter of publication in book form. I can say in complete sincerity that I have bowed reluctantly and with real misgivings to such importunity.

My only possible defense is my valid conviction that the church must constantly address itself to making real and helpful and vital the " faith of our fathers." What the Bible says and what the church has taught historically about God, man, sin, salvation, the person and the work of Jesus Christ, the church of Christ on earth, the preaching of the Word, the sacraments, prayer, and the Holy Spirit must be communicated in understandable language and with relevant emphasis to human minds and hearts in our day and time.

Whether these sermons prove to be an understandable and relevant communication of the Word of God is fortunately not my business to predict! I suspect they will appeal to some and not to others — and for widely divergent reasons in either case. I am bold enough to hope they may be helpful to many lay Christians who want and need assistance in sorting out inherited beliefs which have lost for them the meaning they had for their parents and grandparents. I think they might prove helpful in connection with communicants classes for adults and senior young people seeking to formulate their first profession of faith as new church members.

The sermons entitled " The Means of Grace," " Love and Sacrament," and " The Divine Companion " were excluded by the limitations of the Sundays available from the National Radio Pulpit series. Many of the others have been changed in part or amplified in the treatment accorded them in those broadcasts. All the sermons, however, have been preached to patient and loyal " home congregations," and I am deeply indebted to many fellow Christians in Williamsport, Pennsylvania, Columbus, Ohio, and Pasadena, California, who both by their questions and by their own insights have helped me to think through " the beliefs that matter."

One final word about the title I have selected. I am well aware that it was used many years ago by William Adams Brown as the title for a most helpful book. Also, I am indebted to a noted volume by James S. Stewart for the title of the eighth chapter, " The Strong Name." I understand that it is both legal and ethical to use these titles again. I do so with gratitude. At least *they* cannot be improved upon!

*BELIEFS
THAT
MATTER*

"WHAT DOES IT MATTER?"

Does it matter what we *believe*? A whole generation of Protestant Christians have begun to wonder whether their Christian beliefs are really very important. There is a tendency to say: "Living the Christian life is obviously important, but believing the Christian faith? . . . Well, we're not so sure. What a man *is* counts — definitely; what a man does is crucial; but who cares what a man believes?" We bring Jesus himself into the argument and arraign him on the side of *life* as opposed to *faith*. We have emphasized the Sermon on the Mount as against what we call "theology," failing incidentally to realize that the Sermon on the Mount is itself a creed, a statement of beliefs. Not everybody believes "Happy are the peacemakers," and the reason attached has definite theological implications. So does the Man who said it! The validity of the Beatitudes depends in turn upon what we *believe* about the person who is doing the talking.

Jesus himself put his own first emphasis on the necessity for "belief." At the outset of his ministry, according to Mark's account, he said, "The time is fulfilled and the kingdom of God is at hand; repent, and believe in the gospel"

(Mark 1: 15). The matter of first importance, Jesus said, is belief — not conduct, not a way of life, but how and what to believe.

Actually, the distinction we try to make between life and belief is a completely false one. Belief is essential to life. The old Anglo-Saxon word " belief " literally means " what men live by." " Out of it [the heart] are the issues of life." " As he [a man] thinketh in his heart, so is he." Belief, by definition, is that conviction which conditions decision. It motivates action. It makes me what I am; it impels me to do what I end up doing. How many times have you heard this statement from one of your friends, or perhaps have been guilty of making it yourself in an unguarded moment: " It doesn't make any difference what a man believes so long as he is sincere." But it makes all the difference in the world. And if he believes the wrong thing, the more sincere he is, the more dangerous a man he is. Incidentally, is it not curious and deplorable that this statement is always made about religious beliefs? This means we *believe* that the entire area of religious belief is not important! We never make this kind of statement about belief in any other area of life. For we know that in the areas of conviction that really make a difference to us in life, what a man believes is essential.

Here is a prosecuting attorney. He is examining potential jurors. It is a murder case and he intends to ask for the death penalty. And the first question he addresses to every prospective juror is, " Do you believe in capital punishment? " Because the decision that prospective juror eventually will be called upon to make will be absolutely conditioned by what he believes, and the prosecuting attorney knows it. He knows that if he has a person on the jury who does not believe in capital punishment, he might as well knock his head against a stone wall as to ask that juror to vote for the death penalty, no matter how guilty the man may be proved to be. It is only a matter of belief but it literally " settles the case " — for the juror, the attorneys, and the prisoner at the bar.

Suppose you have a kind farmer friend who wants you to have some of his wonderful fresh milk and thick rich cream. Oh, just one little thing — he doesn't happen to believe in pasteurization! Are you going to drink his wonderfully fresh milk and his nice rich cream? Not if you're in your senses. It's only a matter of his belief, but it can make all the difference to you.

A young couple want to take the weekend off. They have a little child and they need a baby sitter. A fine woman is recommended to them — kind, gentle, reliable — but she doesn't happen to believe in medicine. She fancies herself a faith healer. Now suppose that youngster comes down with an acute attack of appendicitis while they are gone. It's only a matter of belief, but I wouldn't leave my youngster with that woman — I don't care how kind and gentle she may be.

A young man comes courting your attractive, beloved daughter. He is handsome, he has a good job, he has a college education, he has the social graces; but you discover that he doesn't believe in marriage as a permanent relationship. He doesn't happen to believe in the sanctity of the home. Do you want him to marry your daughter? It's only a matter of belief.

Here is an able, brilliant man possessed of all the personality qualifications for leadership in high places, possessed of great intellectual capacity. He occupies a high Government position. The only difficulty is, he happens to be a communist. Does that make any difference to you? It's only a matter of belief! You see, the thing is so silly, this business of saying it doesn't make any difference what a man believes so long as he is sincere. We don't say that in any other area except in the area where we think it doesn't make any difference: religion.

Not so long ago on a TV program I saw a woman who refused to take twenty-five dollars because in order to get it she had to break a mirror. You see, she really believed that breaking a mirror was bad luck. I wish somebody would make that proposition to me, because I would soon be twenty-five dollars richer! The difference between us is a difference of belief. And belief is important. Belief is a conviction which impels or restrains action. Life is made up of acted-out beliefs.

Recently I had occasion to look through a beautifully illustrated book about the signers of our American Declaration of Independence. Now this precious document is a creedal statement. It is a listing of beliefs. I remind you of two phrases, one very near the beginning and one almost the last words in this Magna Charta of American liberties. The beginning of the second paragraph reads: "We hold these truths to be self-evident, that all men are created equal, that they are endowed by their Creator with certain unalienable Rights, that among these are Life, Liberty and the pursuit of Happiness." Here, perhaps, we are not yet talking about true conviction, because it is theoretically possible — indeed it has been demonstrated to be actually true, over and over again — that, intellectually, a man can hold a set of convictions to be self-evident and still do nothing about them. Belief is that which motivates action. Belief determines decision. Belief starts a man doing something. Even "the devils . . . believe, and tremble"; that is, the devils say, "Amen," intellectually, to a certain set of propositions, but they don't really believe, they don't "repent," they don't change their course and find their feet set upon a different pathway because of that to which they are committed in trust. Near the end of the Dec-

laration of Independence, however, there occurs a statement
of real belief. "And, for the support of this Declaration,"
our founding fathers conclude, " with a firm reliance on the
protection of divine Providence, we . . . pledge . . . our
Lives, our Fortunes, and our sacred Honor." That is belief.
If it had not been for that historic belief, there would have
been no American Revolution, and the greatest and freest
nation upon the face of the earth would not now be a national independent entity. It all started with what a few men
believed; it has made all the difference in the world.

Jesus Christ came into the world a special, unique revelation of the will and love of God, and the first thing he said
in public was this: " The time is fulfilled, and the kingdom
of God is at hand [God has entered into human life; his
grace and power are yours for the taking]; repent, and believe." Of many communities in Jesus' lifetime ministry, it
had ultimately and tragically to be said, " He did not do
many mighty works there." Do you remember why? " Because of their unbelief."

What we believe about God makes a lot of difference —
to us, to the world of men lost and afraid, to God himself.
Our souls' sense of security in time and in eternity and the
future of God's Kingdom upon earth depend upon what
you and I believe.

REPENTANCE AND BELIEF

W HY is it so difficult to believe? Because it really is —
for grownups. This is the difference — the lament-
able difference — between an adult and a child. It is a very
hard thing for a grown man really to believe. He knows too
much. He knows too many things that aren't so. And he
knows some things that are so and has lost the capacity to
believe there are any other things that are *more* so, or so in a
different way. He has his little stake in life — he has a partial security, and he refuses to believe there is a larger security
which he will never find until he risks the smaller security.
He depends on himself, and the minute he begins to posit a
faith in somebody else, then in the act he has to give up some
of his self-reliance. He has sold himself a bill of goods to the
effect that his own will and purpose, his own reason, are
what really count in life, and in order really to believe in
something else he has to change this whole point of view. In
other words, he must change his mind about a lot of things.
He has to " repent, and believe." What is this strangely important relationship between repentance and belief? Jesus
stressed it in his first utterance: " The time is fulfilled, and
the kingdom of God is at hand; repent, and believe " (Mark
1: 15).

Repentance is essential to belief. Repentance does not mean, in the first instance, being sorry for your sins. This is frequently involved, but it isn't in itself repentance. Repentance means changing your mind about a lot of admittedly good things in order to believe and appropriate a lot of better things. It isn't just being sorry for your sins. It may mean giving up some of your blessings! The eleventh chapter of The Letter to the Hebrews is replete with the names of heroic men and women who repented and believed. Let's take just one: Exhibit A: Abraham. Abraham, who was called of God to go out not knowing whither he went. This required a tremendous venture of faith upon Abraham's part, and it also involved a lot of repentance. He had to repent of the comfort and security of Ur of the Chaldees. He had to believe that maybe there was a promised land that would look a lot better than Chaldea had ever looked. He had to believe that if he was willing to go out, not knowing whither he went, God would see that he got precisely where he was supposed to go. But first he had to repent of the security he had, the answers he knew, and especially of his own purpose in life. He had to repent of a great many admitted goods, of a good many admitted blessings, before he was ready to believe.

This is a Bible story — it is the story of all true believing, of all real repenting! There came a day when the truth walked up to Christopher Columbus and said: " The world is round. The new route to India lies to the west. Repent and believe." And Christopher Columbus began to repent. That was his virtue. That's why he was a great man. He began to repent of the conviction that the world was flat. He began to repent of the security he had in Spain, and he began to repent of his reputation for having good sense! And as Christopher Columbus and his motley crew sailed out of the bay in those picayune little boats, I am certain a whole group of men stood on the dock cheerily waving them farewell and muttering to each other under their breath, "There goes the damned fool!" They were not swearing, they were saying literally: "There goes a condemned man: condemned physically because, as sure as you were born, he's going to fall off the other edge of the world, which to any man in his right senses is as flat as a pancake. And he is condemned spiritually because he is obviously flying in the face of the will of God, who made the world flat and proposes that we stay on our side of the ocean." You see, the bystanders were in no mood to repent. They were so sure of all the things they knew, and they proposed to hold so tightly to the precious little securities very near and dear to them.

Jesus Christ came into the world, and the first word we hear him saying is, "The time is fulfilled, and the kingdom of God is at hand; repent, and believe in the gospel." What a hard thing to ask any of us to do! We have so much security. We are so completely certain we know all the answers — and the answers we don't know, we're not going to take off of God Almighty or anybody else: "You will have to spell it out for me. I'm from Missouri, spiritually speaking, and I will not repent. I've got to be shown! And if you cannot show me, then I will not believe." It is hard for a grownup to believe, because believing means giving up security and sovereignty; it means to stop making myself and my will and my reason and my intellect and my knowhow the only standard by which I will make a decision in life. Repentance is always involved in belief.

This is true in every area of life. Sometimes my surgeon asks me to repent and believe! He examines me and he says, "You must have a major operation." The first thing I begin to do is to reject that open door to health. He may be a grand fellow, but when it comes to rendering me unconscious and putting me at the mercy of the operating room crew — how do I know whether they know what they're doing? He is asking me to put my little security at the mercy of his concern and his skill and his knowledge and his training. I must now go out not knowing where I'm going, and hope to goodness he knows where he's going and that I'll come back again! This calls for repentance. I shall have to put the government upon his shoulders. I must deny myself and follow him. I am asked to turn and become as a little child; to say: " You know more than I know; you have skill I do not have. I'm convinced you have a high concern for me, that you love me as much as I love myself. O.K., go ahead." That isn't an easy decision to reach. You know it isn't. You must wrestle with the basic issue: how do I get what it takes to repent and believe?

This is the situation in marriage and in the home, is it not? It is hard to *give* yourself *in* a relationship, really to give yourself in love and in trust, because then you give hostages, not to fate, but to some other person. You make a commitment to a relationship. You surrender a very real part of your sovereignty and security. You place yourself at the mercy of this other person — his understanding, her love — and that's a hard thing to do. A lot of people never really do it. I have had a person come in to me and say, " Never again am I going to permit myself to be hurt by that man." Why? Because making a commitment in love does lay you wide open to being hurt. You surrender some security. You are not your own. You can't " call all the shots " in life. You must repent and believe — even admit that there are times when your wife knows as much as you do — maybe a little bit more! This is a hard thing for any man to admit — or any woman, either, for that matter. But is this not Sin with a capital S, this insistence upon my own independence, my own sovereignty? I want to live my own life. I don't want to be beholden to any other person or to any other personal relationship which maybe will push me around when I don't want to be pushed. It is hard to believe in and to give oneself in trust to a relationship that is largely unknown to you, and will only be worked out as you go into it together in faith.

This is our basic difficulty in connection with our belief in God. I do not mean to say there are not individuals who have a sincere intellectual problem in connection with believing in a personal God. But even that intellectual problem, in most instances, is a ramification of this self-love, this inability to deny the self, this determination to make reason the standard, to say that God Almighty has to accommodate himself to my way of looking at things. " The world looks flat to me. I'm not going to take it on faith that it's round, and I'm not willing to experiment to find out if it's round. You say that God is a personal God — and that I shall discover this only as I commit myself in personal trust to him — but I would *rather* think of him as an intangible, abstract mechanical force like electricity. Then I can plug in when I want to, I can plug out when I want to, and I am still in control."

There is intellectual pride involved in this business of rejecting faith in the personal relationship which must exist between God and me. And there is the sinful fear of the loss of personal freedom. Because the minute I really admit God into my life in a personal relationship, that minute a whole chain of decisions and responsibilities is forced upon me. Like my wife, like my children, like my business partner, like my neighbor across the street, like a host of other persons who surround me, God requires something of me. There is a will that may be opposite to my will upon occasion. There is a love which will not let me go but also will not let me off. I must do a lot of repenting before I will believe in the God and Father of Jesus Christ. This basic change is involved: " My reason isn't the only arbiter in this situation; my self-will is not the thing that ultimately counts; my petty, inadequate security is not to be compared with the security that this relationship can offer me." Jesus said, " Unless you turn and become like children [unless you are willing to set aside the things you know that aren't so and the things you know that are so but aren't so *enough*], you will never enter the kingdom of heaven." (Matt. 18: 3.)

Can we see the Kingdom of God at hand in the present flux and turmoil, the chaos and confusion of all our time-honored human relationships? The mold of imperialism is broken once and for all — and the security that this mold held for hundreds of thousands of people is gone with it! The whole world-wide pattern of interracial relationships is breaking up and re-forming almost overnight with all the growing pains inescapably concomitant thereto! Everything that seemed so stable, so assured, so secure, in the Victorian age is as dead as the virtuous and provincial matriarch who gave the age her name. (The very name itself is symbolic of how times have changed. Who would ever think of calling our day the neo-Elizabethan age? The whole center of international and interracial gravity has shifted.)

Does this fact fill us only with fear and foreboding? Or can we discern in the signs of these times the Kingdom of God drawing near? And can we muster the courage to repent and to believe? Why must repentance come so hard, belief be so pathetically weak and witless? Because such repentance and such belief mean setting aside a lot of sovereignty — personal, national, class, race — a lot of security. It means repenting — not of our sins only — but of our prideful reliance upon the " goods " that we have known, which aren't nearly good enough. Jesus Christ came into the world preaching and he said, "The time is fulfilled, the Kingdom of God is at hand — it's yours for the asking and taking — only you must repent, and you'd better start believing." This is a belief that matters.

THE WORD OF GOD

ONE of the most significant editorials that has ever appeared in America was written in the December, 1939, issue of *Fortune*. This editorial said, in part: " Unless we hear a voice, men of this generation will sink down a spiral of depression. There is only one way out of this spiral. The way out is the sound of a voice; not our voice, but a voice coming from something not ourselves in the existence of which we cannot disbelieve. It is the earthly task of the pastors to hear this voice, to cause us to hear it, and to tell us what it says. If they cannot hear it, or if they fail to tell us, we as laymen are utterly lost. Without it we are no more capable of saving the world than we were of creating it in the first place." The question becomes, " Is there such a voice? "

The Christian believes there is: " In many and various ways God spoke of old to our fathers by the prophets; but in these last days he has spoken to us by a Son " (Heb. 1: 1–2). God does speak to man. This is a belief that matters, for upon the Christian doctrine of revelation depends all else in Christian faith and in Christian life. Just as science has its basic assumption, namely, that there is a trustworthy correlation between what a man observes in the universe about him and what is actually out in that universe, so the first article of belief in Christianity is that God speaks and has spoken to the heart of man. In each case it is a matter of belief. You cannot prove it, because every attempt to do so proceeds in the belief you are trying to prove! You can only accept it in faith. God, the unknowable, must choose to reveal himself to me, and the " gospel " is that he has so chosen.

God has spoken in many and various ways. While the Bible is peculiarly, and in a most indispensable sense, the word of God, it is not the only word of God. Jesus himself quoted, " Man shall not live by bread alone, but by *every* word that proceeds from the mouth of God." (Matt. 4: 4.) There is more than one word. Bread — " the staff of life " — is *one* of the words of God. Indeed, the whole universe about us, this physical world of marvel and of beauty is a *word* of God. So the psalmist writes: " The heavens are telling the glory of God; and the firmament proclaims his handiwork. Day to day pours forth speech, and night to night declares knowledge." (Ps. 19: 1–2.) The universe is a " given." It is " there." Man beholds it with his inquiring eye. He examines it with his questing mind, but he did not create it. God said, " Let there be light," or man would never have had that illumination by which he is able to perceive the universe about him.

Reason is another word of God. The capacity to think in orderly fashion, to analyze, to deduce, to discover the laws of this universe by the law of man's reason, to posit theories and establish formulas which are sustained by experiment and observation and logical conclusion — all this is another word of God. It too is a " given." This is the marvel of man: his capacity to think some of God's thought after him. But what man thinks and what man thinks with are alike God's thought. Man discovers God's secrets; he does not make them. Man discovers God's laws; he does not establish them.

Man's reason is an integral part of his being made in the image of God. When he apprehends truth, he apprehends a truth first decreed by Almighty God. Unless God had first said, " Let there be the reasoning mind of man," we should never have known anything about God or ourselves. We should have been as the beasts of the field, which live and perish in ignorance.

Conscience is another word of God: " I ought." Man lives all his life under the shadow of his conscience, which speaks of an authority, of a will, not his own. Whatever other philosophers may think about Immanuel Kant, one thing Kant said still strikes fire in the breast of the common man: " The starry sky above me and the moral law within me alike fill my being with a sense of wonder and of awe." In the universe about us, through the gift of reason, and by the inescapable pull of conscience within us, God has spoken, " Seek ye my face "; and only after the impact of this word, reiterated in varied form and substance, has any man ever responded, " Thy face, Lord, will I seek."

But these words of God are not enough. " In many and various ways God spoke of old to our fathers." The universe speaks of God. It tells us *that* he is. But it cannot tell us who God is. It says, " What hath God wrought! " but it does not tell us his purpose in creating the universe or its lordly tenant, man. It is the difference between the Taj Mahal and the Sphinx. Each speaks of a creative genius, of a conceiving mind, of a skillful hand, but we know why the Taj Mahal was built. To the word of beauty which is implicit in the Taj Mahal itself, its creator has added the explicit word of love: " This is the testimonial of my devotion to my beloved wife." The Sphinx, on the other hand, remains throughout all ages an enigma, wrought in half-intelligible stone. We do not know *why* it was built.

Reason testifies of a God of majesty and order, of law and power, but reason tells me nothing of God's disposition toward me. Does God care? Reason knows no answer to that agonizing plea. The longing of the heart the mind cannot fulfill. Reason is like a sentry parading up and down seeking hopelessly and helplessly to guard the sacrament of personal life, and crying out into the blackness of the void which constantly surrounds us: " Halt! Who goes there, friend or foe? " But reason cannot hear the answer, no matter how hard it may strain. Reason is an orphan child. It can dream about having a father but can never know him.

The voice of conscience is the voice of God, but if conscience is God's last word to me, then I am of all men most miserable. For I discern two strange and tragic facts about conscience. Conscience constantly tells me that I ought, but it cannot tell me *what* I ought to do, nor can it ever give me the grace and power to do it. The word of conscience without the word of grace is a millstone about the neck of a drowning man. So man has always fled the word of conscience, and understandably so, whenever he feared there was no saving word of grace. No man can live with his conscience who has not heard another word of God. The universe, reason, conscience, are words of inestimable value, but they are not words of faith and hope and love. They do not tell me who God is or who I am or what I am to do or how I am to do it. God must tell us more, much more, else we are lost. God has told us more, much more, and we are saved! This is the gospel.

" For God who has spoken to our fathers in many and different ways by the prophets hath in these last days spoken to us by a Son." The Bible is *the* word of God because it contains *this* word of God. It is not about science, or the universe around me. It is about God, the soul of man, and the universe within. It is not a complete, nor a completely accurate, account of human history. The Bible has nothing in common with books such as Darwin's *The Origin of Species* or Gibbon's *Decline and Fall of the Roman Empire.* It simply does not address itself to the problems to which an Einstein devoted his brilliant life or a Churchill his pen of genius. The Bible is God's word about the ultimate issues of life and death, which neither Einstein nor Churchill ever pretended to answer.

The Bible is not therefore without error or distortion or inaccuracy in matters scientific or historical — at the same time it is authoritative and infallible as *the* word of salvation. Let me explain! I have a recording of the great Caruso. The minute you put it on the turntable of a modern high-fidelity phonograph, you realize that when it was recorded, " hi-fi " was not in existence. The recording does not do justice to the immortal voice. And through the years the record itself has suffered some damage. When you play it, you are conscious of the surface scratches as well as of the original distortion, but you still know you are listening to possibly the greatest tenor voice this world has ever heard. This is the *important* thing about that record. You are not supposed to worship the record anyhow! You are supposed to listen to the voice.

So the Bible speaks of God as our Father, of man as God's child — of man as God's wayward, self-seeking, sinful child, from Adam to the prodigal son. The Bible speaks of God's purpose in human history to establish a fellowship, to create a family of those who return his love with an answering love for God and for their neighbor. The Bible speaks of the infinite patience and the everlasting love of God for his children, of the pain which he endures in the face of their selfishness, of the suffering which he shares with them, suffering that they bring upon themselves through their own sins, suffering that God takes upon himself because he will not forsake his children even when they turn their backs upon him. The Bible speaks of the life that is in God, that stems from God, which he desires to give to his children at infinite cost to himself. The Bible speaks of a personal relationship possible between you and God, and me and God, and you and me *in* God, which when once embraced cannot be destroyed by sin or death itself. This revelation came through the centuries to men and through men who had personal experiences of God in daily life — men like Abraham, Moses, David, Elijah, Isaiah, the eighth-century prophets — culminating in Jesus Christ, the Word of God made flesh, the Son fashioned in the express image of the Father, full of grace and truth.

We have other phonograph records in our collection — recent records — compiled and edited by Edward R. Murrow, entitled " I Can Hear It Now." They recapture the voices of men and leaders of men who participated in the agonizing and the triumphant events of our contemporary world. The Bible is also like that. It is the voice of God, the saving word of the gospel of Jesus Christ. And I can hear it now! This is the voice not our voice. Do we believe that it is speaking, and are we listening? One of the great historical novels of this generation, and one too little read, is a novel by Franz Werfel based upon the life of the prophet Jeremiah and entitled *Hearken Unto the Voice*. This is the plea of the Bible, this is the plea of the Voice itself: " Hear, that your soul shall live."

Jesus Christ neared his last hour in human flesh upon this earth overborne and overwrought in spirit because of the unwillingness of sinful man to hear and heed: " How often would I have gathered your children together as a hen

gathers her brood under her wings, and you would not! "
(Matt. 23: 37.) How does a hen seek to gather her chickens
under her wing? She *clucks* to them. She calls to them in a
language that is their own, which they are supposed to understand. They do not answer because they will not *listen*.
Jesus Christ, the " good shepherd," voices the high and holy
and ardent hope that when he calls, his sheep, knowing his
voice and hearing themselves called each one by name, will
heed and follow. You and I, as the *Fortune* editorial truly
prophesied, have no other recourse than to go down a spiral
of everlasting depression unless we hear a voice not our
voice. And that voice is the voice of God in Jesus Christ, the
word of God made flesh.

To what voice do you choose to listen? " Lord, to whom
shall we go? You have the words of eternal life." (John
6: 68.) " To-day if ye will hear his voice, harden not your
heart." (Ps. 95: 7–8.) This is a belief that matters.

GOD THE FATHER ALMIGHTY

O NE of the more impelling plays that graced the Broad-
way stage a couple of seasons ago was *The Lark*, a
gripping dramatization of the life of Joan of Arc. Joan of Arc
was a girl whose life was qualified and conditioned and moti-
vated by a consummate and consuming belief in what she
called her "Voices." Now one cannot believe *in* a "Voice"
without believing in what the "Voice" has to say. This was
the kind of belief Joan had, and this belief gave her, not a
philosophy for pious contemplation — it did not make her
happier or more secure — but rather an understanding of
life and of the part she had to play in it. In the confusion
and danger of the world of her day, she came to know what
she had to do, and what she heard led her into conflict with
the dauphin, with the French nobles, with the English, and,
before she was through, with the church of which she was
a member, by which she was judged, excommunicated, and
ultimately destroyed. All this happened, not because she believed in something *about* God, but because she believed *in*
God — in the God who confronts every man with a declaration of sovereignty over that man's life, a sovereignty that is
superior to all lesser sovereignties, be they king or country,
family or church, or the infinitely lesser sovereignties of

personal predilection and desire. To Joan of Arc the language and meaning of the word of God about himself was absolutely real: " I am the Lord *your* God " (Ex. 20: 2).

This kind of belief is fundamental to the doctrine of Christian revelation. So the first article of the Apostles' Creed reads: " I believe in God the Father Almighty." This does not mean, " I believe God exists." It does mean, " I believe God exists for me; I believe in the God who confronts me." It was what the psalmist believed when he wrote, " O God, thou art *my* God." Lots of people say, " I believe in God, and this is my idea of him." They then go on to settle for an idea of God that does not affect to the slightest degree their relationship either with God or with their neighbors. Voltaire, in describing his inadequate relationship to God, said, " We bow, but we do not speak." As a " deist," Voltaire believed in the existence of God as a fact without relevance to human life. Such a purely intellectual acceptance of the existence of God means literally nothing. It makes no difference at all.

I believe in the existence of Mt. Everest. I really do. But all my believing about Mt. Everest doesn't involve me or my daily life in any way. I have a very comfortable faith about Mt. Everest. I can take it or leave it, and most of the time, brother, I prefer to let it strictly alone. Even if I saw it, the only thing I could ever *do* about it would be to climb it, and that I most assuredly should not want to do. This is the way many people believe about God. They have a curiosity about him. Maybe they would like to see him — at not too close quarters — someday, but they are neither ready nor willing to do the things that might be incumbent upon them if they ever came to grips with the God revealed in the Bible. Theirs is a Mt. Everest kind of belief. God becomes a matter for speculation and investigation for those interested in that kind of thing. As for theologians, well, they may be as intrepid in their field as mountain climbers, though somewhat less understandable and probably less admirable.

We talk *about* God endlessly; he is like a dying man stretched out in a kind of deathlike coma upon his bed. We cannot talk to him; he certainly cannot talk back to us — we hope — and it is therefore perfectly permissible and safe to talk *about* him in the sickroom which he occupies, speculating about his chances for survival.

Or we wait around for the scientists to count the atomic ballots for or against God. Take this quotation: " I believe in God because of the evidence of science. There was until recently a notion that there was a conflict between science and religion . . . because science tried to prove there was no God. Science has never tried any such foolish thing. It is a search for truth; God is truth, so there can be no conflict. God does not have to fear investigation; he asks for it." There is a sense in which this is so. But there is a very dangerous sense in which it isn't so at all. God does not ask for investigation. God asks to be heard! He is not a theorem in geometry. He is not a metaphysical frog stretched out upon some cosmic laboratory table. He is not an object of research. I certainly agree that true science has never tried any such foolish thing as to attempt to disprove God. But there are many foolish scientists and a great many foolish nonscientists who believe that the only possible God is the God who *could* be proved by so-called " scientific " investigation. Human reason is at the height and the end of its folly when it enters into the field of speculative philosophy with a kind of metaphysical Geiger counter and comes out with the reassuring report, " It is now intellectually safe for you to go in and begin believing in God."

For Voltaire and all the little voltaires — and their name

is legion — are dead wrong about God. We may pass God by — he will permit us so to do — bowing and never speaking, but *God does not pass us by and he does not stop speaking!* When Columbus walked up to the sailors of Lisbon, saying: " The world is round. Come with me and let us discover the new route to the East by sailing west," he was raising an issue that debate could never settle. By settling for debate rather than for sailing with Columbus, the vote was cast for disbelief. So it is with God.

This is why the Biblical approach to God is so entirely different. The Bible has nothing to say to the man who wants to settle for: " This is what I think about God. What do you think? " The Bible starts out slam-bang: " This is God talking: ' I am the Lord your God.' What do you propose to do about it? " This changes the whole situation. The man from the prairies who has never seen the ocean can still speculate about what the ocean is like if he wants to. But the swimmer battling in a raging surf can only affirm with Francis Thompson, " That Voice is round me like a bursting sea " (*The Hound of Heaven;* The Newman Press; used by permission). God is not patiently waiting in some far-off cosmic reception room while human reason examines his credentials line upon line and precept upon precept and perhaps finally with royal graciousness extends the scepter of intellectual acceptance and beckons God into the throne room where man sits in sovereign power. God is already in the throne room! — and upon the throne. He summons man for the royal interview, and begins that interview, " I am the Lord your God." And he waits for my reply!

Once that Voice is heard, the activity required is not primarily intellectual; it is moral. It is an act of the will. It is not, " What am I to *think* about this God? " It is rather, " Lord, what wilt thou have me to do? " God does not come in to me to sit for a portrait which is utterly beyond my capacity to paint. Neither the brush of intellect nor the brush of intuition can avail; I have no colors on my palette that are suitable to paint the picture of God. God comes in, as he came to Ezekiel of old, and he says, " Son of man, stand upon your feet, and I will speak with you."

The words of our text are immediately followed by the Ten Commandments. That is not an accident. The only be- lief in God that matters is the response of our hearts to *what* God has to say. The child Samuel, in the darkness of his own adolescent experience and in the darkness of the Temple, began to grasp the truth that there was a will not his own which was making for righteousness and a Voice that he had to do something about. He went to Eli and said, " What am I to do? ", and Eli, who knew God, advised the boy, " You'd better say, ' Speak, Lord, for thy servant hears.' " But this is just what we don't want God to do, and this is why we do not want to believe in the God who speaks. Once we believe that, we have to listen and we have to respond.

So the Children of Israel were not at all happy when Moses brought back to them from Mt. Sinai what God had said — the Ten Commandments! They bustled up to Moses and they started imploring: " Now, Moses, you tell us what it's all about because we can't stand to listen to what God has to say. Maybe we can take what you have on your mind. You tell us what you think about God, and then you let us tell you what we think about God, and maybe we can work this thing around so that we shall all like to listen to what we all like to think God is up to."

This is Sin. This is Sin with a capital S. Man is not willing to believe in the only kind of God there is because he cannot bear to listen to what God has to say. He can't take it! There are hundreds of thousands of people in this world who are engaged in running around buttonholing this teacher and that prophet and their next-door neighbor and everybody they can lay their hands on and proposing, " Now let's sit down and think about God, and let's decide what God is like, and whether we like what he is like, and whether we feel like doing what he wants us to do." So all the whims and fancies, the sects and philosophies, the false prophets and the " Athenians " lead sinful man astray in his vanity, pride, and fear. " The stars will tell us; our glands will tell us; this fellow will tell us; somebody else will tell us . . . what we like to hear and what maybe we feel like doing."

And all the while God stands over us, each and every one, saying, " I am the Lord your God." The God who has alike the first and last word of creative power and sovereign purpose is the only God there is to believe in. Fortunately for us, God also speaks the saving word of love! God never speaks and asks us to do something without also speaking again and giving us what it takes to do it, including forgiveness for our initial unwillingness to listen and to try! Moses sought to reassure the Children of Israel because Moses had talked with God, and he knew that God talks with a man " face to face, as a man speaks to his friend." Would you know more about God than you know now? There is only one way: " He that doeth the will of God shall know the teaching." But first things come first. You will not know what his will is for you until you believe the first word he has to say: " I am the Lord your God." This is a belief that matters.

THE SOVEREIGNTY OF GOD

Sᴏᴍᴇ facts in life are "sovereign"; their very existence requires a subordinate action from me. As already pointed out, Mt. Everest is *not* such a sovereign fact; a brush fire racing down to engulf my home *is*. Mt. Everest will let me alone and I can retaliate in kind, but the fire will not let me alone, and so I have to do something about it. It is a sovereign fact.

Personal relationships in life are sovereign facts. My covenant relationship to my wife is such a sovereign fact. In love, it controls not only my attitude and my behavior toward her, but also my attitude and my behavior toward all other members of the so-called "fair sex"! The relationship of a citizen to the United States of America is a sovereign relationship. "I pledge allegiance to the flag of the United States of America" because of "the Republic for which it stands, one nation, under God, indivisible, with liberty and justice for all." Millions of men and women and young people have entered into free covenant relationships with one another, establishing free institutions by the method of a free electorate in which each one of us pledges to abide by the will of the majority. It is a sovereign relationship because it is a covenant relationship.

Now for Christians one of the beliefs that matters is this: A man's relationship to God is the supremely sovereign relationship. It qualifies, controls, and activates all other relationships, allegiances, and truths. Jesus Christ himself gave the everlasting "Amen" to the sovereignty of God when he quoted the Old Testament in resisting his own temptation to live apart from that sovereignty: "You shall worship the Lord your God, and him only shall you serve" (Luke 4:8). According to the Bible, this sovereign relationship to God reveals itself in three categories of personal experience.

First of all, there is the sovereignty of God's *creative* love. "I believe in God the Father Almighty, Maker of heaven and earth. . . ." God is my Father, and as such he sustains a sovereign covenant relationship to me, his child. So Jesus Christ in telling the moving story of the prodigal son represents God the Father giving to man, his child, life and the things needful for the sustenance of life, and represents the son as gladly acknowledging this sovereignty of giving. He *accepts* the gift of life — he can do no other — and with selfish greed he lays hold upon his patrimony: "Father, give me the share of property that falls to me!" *In so asking* he acknowledges the sovereign grace of his Father, who can give or withhold as he will.

God the Father also has a holy "design for living" which he gives to his son; which he *owes* to his son out of his wisdom and his grace. Best and greatest and most dangerous of all, he gives to man, his beloved child, freedom whereby to appropriate the design for living and thus enter into an everlasting fellowship with his Father. But while the child is willing to say "Amen" to part of this sovereign relationship, he refuses to say "Amen" to the rest of it. He accepts the material inheritance, but rejects the design for living. He appropriates the gift of freedom and says no to God's sovereignty over the rest of his life. He goes into the far country, there to live alone and try to like it.

But every lesser freedom man demands — personal, political, economic, and social — stems from and is rooted in his freely remaining in this sovereign covenant-keeping relationship with God, the source of all freedom. When man uses his freedom to live apart from the sovereignty of God, he winds up every single time serving some man-made, spurious sovereignty of czar or pope, of prince or priest, of this or that dictator. The worst dictator of all can be " demos " unrestrained, the rule of the mob! None of these are covenant relationships, and therefore none of them are sovereign. There is no integrity in them; performance can never follow promise; they are not rooted in love; the service they require is slavery and the ultimate gift they bestow is death. Only God in creative love can offer the sovereign covenant-keeping relationship that is " Yea and Amen "; only God proposes to keep the covenant made in love unto life everlasting; only God offers the service that is perfect freedom. " You shall worship the Lord your God, and him only shall you serve."

In his attempt to escape God's sovereign creative love, man experiences the sovereignty of God's reconciling, redeeming love. You see, God does not propose to let man " get away with it." The son proposes to lose his identity in the far country and the father will not have it so. The boy may fondly believe that he can use his freedom to escape out of the sovereign love of God, but, because it is sovereign and covenant-keeping, it will follow him to the uttermost ends of this earth. This is the mystery — the true and abiding and saving mystery — of the cross of Jesus Christ. For in the cross God at one and the same time says, " No," in an outraged, everlasting protest against the escape sought in the far country even while he says, " Yes," to the boy himself in love and forgiveness. The cross of Jesus Christ is God's terrible indictment of the reality of his child's waywardness and sin of rejection. It is God's everlasting refusal to call man's " black " God's " white," but it is also God's everlasting, agonizing plea to his wayward child to come home. With outstretched, nail-pierced hands, he holds open the door of home for the returning prodigal.

Read again the parable of the prodigal son and note that Jesus does not represent the father as writing a grandfatherly, namby-pamby type of letter to this boy, saying: " Hope you are enjoying your well-deserved vacation. Understand you are running low on funds. Enclosed please find check! " He lets the boy " stew in his own juice " because he cannot condone either the far country or his boy's being there. But on that welcome day when the boy's figure darkens the far horizon, the father's heart rejoices with exceeding great joy and he rushes to meet him because he has never stopped loving the boy and has never stopped exercising upon that boy's mind and heart the influences of his reconciling spirit. This is the sovereignty of God's redemptive love, taking the initiative in reconciliation even as he takes it in creation, revealing to lost and guilty and sinful man the only way of salvation, the only way back home. So God in Jesus Christ speaks through this " Word . . . made flesh," *the* word of reconciling love. The Bible says that you and I simply dare not worship or serve any other God than this God whose sovereign purpose in forgiveness is to save us from our sins. " You shall worship the Lord your God, and him only shall you serve."

Christians also experience the sovereign exercise of God's guiding love. God does not leave man to his own devices. Over and over again, we wish he would, but he will not let us alone. Man, the lost child of God, remains truly lost unless

God maintains his sovereign purpose to guide him and to influence him "into all truth." If we are wise and loving parents, long before our children are able to make conscious choices for themselves, in parental love we have conditioned those children. We have brought to bear upon their lives, through precept and example, through training and education, through the relentless pressure of ideals and concepts, an induced fellowship with the good, the true, and the beautiful in life; we have already molded them so that their choices, without ever overruling their freedom, are determined. No parent worthy of the name says to the child, "Do this because I say so," but no parent worthy of the name of love refuses to extend to his child the sovereign guidance of that love.

Here is found the significance of the sacrament of infant Baptism for many Christians. In such a sacrament fathers and mothers say, "We propose to keep faith with our children by conditioning their choices through every legitimate means at our command, just as we believe God exercises the sovereignty of his guiding love upon all of us — his children." In Jesus' story of the prodigal son, all that the father had ever sought to impress upon that wayward boy in the formative years was ceaselessly at work in the tortured soul of that lad while he was floundering in the far country. While he was struggling to find himself, every unseen, seemingly unfelt, pressure of his father's continuing love was working upon his mind and soul. After he returned home, the "growing pains" which were an inescapable part of his reidentifying himself consciously with the guiding love of his father constituted the "homework" which insured that ultimately he would grow in grace and enter into a renewed fellowship with his father.

Man is free to deny God's purpose in his life, but man is

not ever free from the sovereign pressure of the Holy Spirit
— the *Holy* Spirit, the Spirit who everlastingly seeks to re-
establish wholeness and unity *within* a man, *between* a man
and his rejected Father, *between* a man and his rejected
brother. We live under the sovereignty of the guiding love of
God, and man's only salvation from the tragic effect of seeking to do that which is right in his own eyes is to be found
in accepting the sovereignty of the Holy Spirit, who will
and does lead men and women back to God, and back to
one another in a fellowship of faith and service. " You shall
worship the Lord your God, and him only shall you serve."

Have you realized that we have been thinking about the
doctrine of the Trinity? The Trinity is not a " dogma," the
intellectual apprehension of which is essential to the soul's
salvation. Salvation depends upon our hearing the God who
presents his sovereign claim with a trinity of voices. The
Trinity is not a problem in celestial arithmetic; it is not a
metaphysical " Chinese puzzle "; it represents the inadequate
formulation of the facts of human experience confronted
with the sovereignty of God. Centuries ago the psalmist pro-
claimed his unswerving belief in the triune reality of God
when he exulted, " The Lord of hosts is with us; the God of
Jacob is our refuge " (Ps. 46: 11). " The Lord of hosts " —
God the Father Almighty, in all his panoply of grace and
power, bearing gifts unto us, his children, upon which we
are completely and solely dependent — this sovereign God is
part and parcel of our contemporary experience; he is with
us in the power and presence of his Holy Spirit; and " the
God of Jacob " — the saving God, the God who with agonizing patience " puts up with " Jacob, the prototype of sinful,
self-willed man, outlasting his arrogance and his greed, finally " touching " him so that he limps through life in testimony to the power of God's humbling forgiveness, and

through that mysterious experience becomes a prince of God and reconciled to his brother, Esau — this " God of Jacob," who became incarnate in Jesus Christ, is also " our refuge and strength." " Warm, sweet, tender, even yet A present help is He; And faith has still its Olivet, And love its Galilee." (John G. Whittier.)

"You shall worship the Lord your God, and him only shall you serve." This is a belief that matters.

"WHAT IS MAN?"

THE most important question in the universe, apart from the question, "What is God?" is the question, "What is man?" The Bible is the record of men in every generation who have found the same answer to this basic question. "What is man that thou art mindful of him? . . . Thou hast made him little less than God, and dost crown him with glory and honor." (Ps. 8: 4–5.) The Bible begins with this same tremendous assertion of the high and unique character of man when it states unequivocally, "So God created man in his own image." Man's nature is rooted in his inescapable relationship to God; he bears within himself the hallmark of the divine.

The very question itself reveals the peculiar nature of man amid all of God's marvelous creation. Man alone is self-conscious! Man alone *can* ask such a question. More significant still, he *must* ask it. He cannot keep from asking it. He everlastingly asks it. "What is man? Who am I?" This is his nature. To paraphrase one of the current advertising slogans, "No other animal can ask this question!" This is the universal concern of man alone.

Why is it that every young man, usually somewhere in his college career, begins to wrestle with this question? "Who am I? What am I meant to do with my life?" The young tiger never troubles himself with such questions. He doesn't even know he is a tiger, therefore he doesn't have to decide whether he is going to be a good tiger or a bad tiger, or what kind of vocation he will go into as a tiger. The idea never dawns upon the tiger that he has any freedom of choice or that, conversely, he has any sense of responsibility. This is the difference between a tiger and a man. A man always knows he is a man, and therefore he cannot escape asking the fundamental question about his manhood. He *has* a sense of freedom. He *has* a sense of responsibility. They are the opposite sides of the spiritual coin which is his patrimony. All the big decisions in life that a man alone must make, which alternately exalt and terrify him, are required of him because of his unique nature. *Because* he is a man, he must think, he must choose, he must decide. In the language of Charles Wesley's familiar hymn, a man must " wrestle and fight and pray; Tread all the powers of darkness down, And win the well-fought day." This is his peril. This is his power. He is a man — that's the way he's made.

Will you note also that the question itself, " What is man?", really means, " To whom am I related, as a man?" A man only finds out who he is by finding out to whom he belongs. I once read a story about a victim of amnesia. He had lost his memory as the result of a bus accident. The only clue he possessed concerning his identity was the bus ticket he found within his vest pocket. He went back to the starting point which the ticket revealed to him he had used in getting on the bus, hoping to find someone back at the beginning of his journey who would know him, to whom he belonged. He found he had a wife and two lovely children. He found he had a business and a business partner. He found he had a host of friends. He rediscovered who he was by rediscovering to whom he belonged. So in the Bible the everlasting answer to the question, " What is man? ", is found by going back to the beginning of the journey of life and rediscovering: " *God created man in his own image.*" *Man belongs to God.*

Man's unique relationship as over against the rest of God's animal creation has been beautifully described in James Weldon Johnson's moving paraphrase of the Genesis story of creation:

> " Then God walked around,
> And God looked around
> On all that he had made.
> He looked at his sun,
> And he looked at his moon,
> And he looked at his little stars;
> He looked on his world
> With all its living things,
> And God said, ' *I'm lonely still.*'

> " Then God sat down
> On the side of a hill where he could think;
> By a deep, wide river he sat down;
> With his head in his hands,
> God thought and thought,
> Till he thought, ' *I'll make me a man!* '

> " Up from the bed of the river
> God scooped the clay;
> And by the bank of the river
> He kneeled him down;
> And there the great God Almighty
> Who lit the sun and fixed it in the sky,
> Who flung the stars to the most far corner of the night,
> Who rounded the earth in the middle of his hand;
> This Great God,
> Like a mammy bending over her baby,

Kneeled down in the dust
Toiling over a lump of clay
Till he shaped it in his own image;

"Then into it he blew the breath of life,
And man became a living soul."

("The Creation," in *God's Trombones.* Copyrighted by
The Viking Press, Inc., 1927. Used by permission.)

Now forget the notion that this story — either in the original Genesis record or in Mr. Johnson's matchless paraphrase
of it — ever pretended to be a scientific account of *how* God
created man. If you ever thought that, stop thinking it. It
tells an infinitely more important truth, one that science
knows nothing about. It tells us *why* God created man —
and *what* God created man. "God created man in his own
image."

God created man *in love,* to "think God's thoughts after
him." God endowed man with reason and with conscience;
with an infinite and eternal capacity for the love of the good,
the true, the beautiful in life. God gave to man in love a
goodly proportion of his own creative powers. Most important of all, God bequeathed to man — in love — such a sufficiency of his own sovereignty that man might freely choose
to accept his high destiny as a child of God and to enter into
such a fellowship of love and of service as would alike make
glad the heart of his Creator and minister to his own abiding happiness and peace. God built into man at the very core
of his nature a deep and quenchless yearning, a hunger for
a fellowship of the Spirit, which the things of earth and the
most intimate association with all other "creatures" could
never completely satisfy. Man, like God, is a moral spirit who
hungers and thirsts after righteousness — the right relation-

ships with other moral, spiritual beings which are possible
to man alone.

In Jesus' story of the two sons, there was a world of difference in the relationship between the father and his sons, and
between the father and his flocks and his herds and his slaves.
The relationship between the father and the child is an alto-
gether different relationship from that existing between the
father and every other *thing* that he possesses. The father-
child relationship is based upon a kinship between the son
and the father. The boy not only looks like his father — he
will someday, pray God, act like his father if he chooses to
remain in fellowship with his father. " Son, you are always
with me, and all that is mine is yours." (Luke 15: 31.) This
is man's spiritual endowment, for God created man in his
own image.

We must note most carefully that " God *created* man."
Man is utterly unique among all of created life — but, as a
" creature," man can no more change his basic nature than
can any other creature. Man has a rich spiritual endowment
which carries with it a large measure of freedom and responsibility, but man is not completely free. He cannot
change his relationship to God. He cannot deny his birthright; he cannot escape his " sonship."

Let us put it this way: Our own son is " our son " as long
as he lives. For better or for worse, his freedom — which
is real and substantial — can never permit him to renounce
the fact of his sonship. He may use this freedom to try to
escape the privileges and the responsibilities of that basic
relationship, but he cannot change the relationship itself. He
cannot alter the fact. He can never escape out of his created
nature as our son. Nor can he find happiness, nor any degree
of spiritual security, in the vain attempt.

Now if I had a rabbit — which, praise the Lord, I do not

have—he also in a very real sense would be "my rabbit," but he would have no such freedom or responsibility as has my son. If he runs away from home, he is not denying his own nature or violating his nonexistent freedom or responsibility. He is just being a rabbit. But when a boy runs away from home, he is attempting the impossible—the denial of his nature, the misuse of his freedom, the renouncing of his birthright, the disclaiming of his responsibilities. He is not that free!

The sin and sorrow and tragedy of man's life is refusal to acknowledge that he is *made in the image of God*. He will not accept the fact that he is a "creature." He likes to fool himself into thinking that he can become *as* God, and so escape out of any dependence upon God as his Father. This was Adam's sin in the Garden. This is your sin and mine. This is the tragedy of all human sin. Man was so created that he is forever dependent upon his Father's grace and love. Man is free to choose, for love that is compelled is never love, and service that is enforced is not service—it is slavery. But whenever man, the child of God, chooses to love himself alone, or chooses to serve some other God than the Heavenly Father who made him for Himself, man is attempting to deny his own nature—the impossible—and will find no adequate substitute relationship among all the created wonders of his Father's universe.

Man is free to rebel as the animal is not free. I repeat, the tiger is a tiger—period! He must obey the law of God governing "tigerhood." But man is also subject to a most high and holy law of love for God, which governs his manhood. Man's nature is such that he may be free to rebel, but he is not free to find fulfillment in that rebellion. Man is free to choose whom he will serve, but, being a creature and not God, he is not free to choose *not to serve* at all. This again was Adam's sin — the sin of the denial of his dependence upon God, the denial of his creaturehood in disloyal response to the fond fancy whispered in his ear, " Ye shall be as gods " (Gen. 3:5).

This was the sin of the prodigal son: " Father, give me the share of property that falls to me." " If only I can lay hands upon my father's goods, that, plus my own goodness, will be good enough." He found out that he had not been so created. And when he finally came to himself and found, hidden deep within, the lost image of his father, he knew what he had to do: " I will arise and go home, to my father to whom I belong and in whose love alone I can become a man! "

This is the story of the Bible from cover to cover. This is the voice of God pleading through his servants and his prophets in every generation. Joshua cries to the Children of Israel, " Choose this day whom you will serve." But you must serve somebody. Such is man's nature as a creature of God's love. Elijah exhorts, " If the Lord is God, follow him; but if Baal, then follow him." But man must follow somebody. That is his created nature. Jesus Christ pleads, " You cannot serve God and mammon." But you must serve one. Only the fool says in his heart, " There is no God." The " fool " is always a man who would deny his birthright, his destiny, and his dependence. We cannot escape out of the relationship given classic definition by the great Augustine: " Thou hast made us for thyself, and our hearts are restless until they find their rest in thee." For " so God created man in his own image." This is a belief that matters.

THE REALITY OF SIN

IT does not seem very constructive to say, "I believe in sin," but this is one of the beliefs that matter. A man has no business putting his faith in his doctor's suggested cure unless he is certain of the accuracy of his doctor's diagnosis. It is all right for my doctor to recommend to me " pink pills for pale people " if my only difficulty is that my blood is a little below par. But if, in fact, I have leukemia, while I may not like to hear him tell me so, I want him to diagnose it correctly, and and then I want just as many blood transfusions as I can get. We must face up to the reality of sin because the gospel of Jesus Christ is a complete irrelevance apart from this grim fact.

The story of the Fall of man in Genesis is an allegory, but it is the truest story ever told because it reminds us that man has a fatal spiritual disease which is called Sin — with a capital S. The fall of Adam did not occur a long, long time ago only. Adam means " Man." Adam is " Everyman." And the fall of Adam is Everyman's fall. The story of Adam is your story and mine.

It is the story of man, made in the image of God, created the child of God, and all too soon a rebel without cause! He suffers delusions of grandeur. He will not serve either as a

steward or as a son. " Man in Revolt " is not only the title of
a familiar book; it is the sad saga of man's agelong relationship to God his Father. Man is Absalom to God's David;
man is David to God's Uriah; man is Ahab to God's Naboth;
man is Judas to God's Christ. Man is never content to sit in
the " House of Commons "; he insists in moving over to the
" House of Lords "! Everyman is the " Man Who Would Be
King." This is his disease. This is his delusion. This is Sin.
The essence of Sin is man's use of his freedom under God to
exalt himself to the throne of God. And the serpent said to
Eve — and Eve to Adam, nothing loath — " Ye shall be
as gods " (Gen. 3:5). So Nietzsche put into the mouth of
Zarathustra, " If there were gods, who could endure not to
be one? " Certainly not man! Man is forever fooling himself
into believing that he can in fact be free only if he owes his
life to himself. All man's " sins " — with a small " s " — are
rooted in this Sin.

We must emphasize also that Sin is spiritual in its origin
— not physical. Pride, the father of Sin, is of the spirit and
not of the flesh. My sin springs out of that part of me which
is akin to God, not that part of me which is akin to the rest
of the animal creation. Sin is not my lower nature warring
against my higher nature. Sin is my higher nature in rebellion against God. " Original sin " simply means that sin mys-
teriously, fatally, is regnant in the spiritual side of your life
and mine. It is " original " in each and every one of us. No
man who pretends to be half honest can deny the truth:
" None is righteous, no, not one; no one understands, no one
seeks for God. All have turned aside, together they have gone
wrong; no one does good, not even one " (Rom. 3: 11–12).

Moreover, sin not only enslaves all men but *all of* a man.
There is a tragic irony in our human situation. Pascal calls
the turn: " In preferring himself to God, and in refusing

divine grace, man has truly lost himself. He is become, to the very roots of his will, the slave to the 'me' that has hypnotized him" (*Pascal,* by Emile Cailliet, pp. 161–162; The Westminster Press). Seeking to escape out of the service of God his Father, man finds himself enslaved to the very elements within himself that he was meant to rule under God: he becomes a slave to his own animal nature. I repeat that "original sin" — man's prideful separation from God — is of the spirit, not of the flesh. But once the spirit of man has denied its dependence upon God, then it loses its independence to the flesh, and man's animal nature "takes over." That which was meant to serve begins to rule, with the result that sinful man does "animal-like" things that no decent animal would ever think of doing. Sinful man "drinks like a fish"; only the fish doesn't. Sinful man "eats like a hog"; but a hog doesn't. The drug addict gets "hopped up like a rabbit"; but the rabbit doesn't. Man "makes like a wolf"; but the wolf doesn't. Man declares himself free from the service of God, and he becomes the slave of his glands. The Bible puts it naïvely, obliquely, with becoming taste: " Then the eyes of both were opened, and they knew that they were naked "; and they were ashamed! (Gen. 3:7).

Man's sin enslaves him to his own "reason." Nothing is more characteristic of sinful man than the inescapable necessity which he finds himself under to deify his "reason." He can no longer believe anything his "reason" tells him he must not believe. He cannot accept any relationship his "reason" instructs him is inimical to his own vaunted independence. His "reason," which was meant to be the servant of his faith in God, has now become the tyrant that tells him he may no longer believe in God! "Reason" exalted to the throne immediately exercises "thought control," and it warns man against the subversive idea that he is meant to serve God. "Reason" becomes the "people's court," the court of last inquiry, which, summarily and out of hand, denies the existence of God. Moreover, the tyrant "Reason" now dictates to sinful man what is "goodness" and what is "love"—what are good and loving relationships in life. It is no longer what God thinks or what God says or what God demonstrates to be both good and loving. It is a matter of what is now "reasonable" for man.

The Sermon on the Mount is most certainly not "reasonable"; the kind of love that God has manifested in Jesus Christ is not reasonable, therefore man, the slave of reason, will have none of it. Sinful man is no longer able or willing to "think God's thoughts after him." "Reason" forbids it, either in faith or in life.

Not only does sinful man find himself enslaved to his infected reason and to his rebellious flesh; his mania for mastery enslaves him over and over again to the freely accepted tyranny of his fellow man. This sounds like a contradiction in terms, but the sordid pages of history are compact with reiterated examples. Ancient Irael walks up to Samuel, servant of God and servant of the people, and implores, "Give us a king to govern us." We want a dictator! Why? So that he may lead us out to victorious battle and we can become masters over our neighbors. Every dictator the history of the world has ever known has ridden to power over his fellow sinners with the spurious promise, "Surrender your liberty to me, and I will make you top dog!" This was the false hope held out by Hitler with his "Nordic supremacy" and his "Pan-Germanism." This is the equally spurious promise of communism, with its "dictatorship of the proletariat": "Be *some*body's slave, and you will become master over *every*body else!"

So sinful man becomes willing to surrender his freedom

to king and prelate. Denying the sovereignty of God in his life, he becomes a " sinful sucker " — wide open to some fellow sinner, who, with equal passion to rule and with more ingenuity and energy, enslaves his sinful brethren in their millions. Sinners all, by our own choice, " as sheep having no shepherd," we become fair game for the first iron-fisted sheepherder who comes along. Sinful man is always willing and eager to believe that he can be " king " or " queen " for a day, and so he surrenders his freedom to someone who enslaves him for the rest of his life.

The final and awful measure and scope of man's enslavement to Sin is seen in what " good " and " reasonable " sinful men did to Jesus Christ, the Son of Man and the Son of God — the supreme demonstration of what God intended man to be, the complete revelation of what God is. We must face the truth: Jesus Christ was crucified by the best sinful men on earth: the scribes, the Pharisees, the philosophers, the theologians, the judges, the maintainers of law and order, the preservers of the peace. He was condemned to death in the name of law and order, in the name of " reason," in the name of " religion." You see, sinful man prefers his own sinful ways to the ways of God. " My thoughts are not your thoughts, neither are your ways my ways, says the Lord." (Isa. 55: 8.) This is " total depravity " — sin infects all of a man.

Sin alienates man from God, and it ought to alienate God from man. My sin creates a barrier between me and God. I can erect the barrier, but I have no power to tear it down. " All we like sheep have gone astray." Like silly sheep, we have wandered off and fallen into a deep ravine, and we cannot stumble out; we are caught in a thicket, and we cannot disentangle ourselves. But it is more even than that. It is partly that we do not *want* to get back with sufficient spiritual energy actually to fight our way back. So Paul, out of his own experience, can write of the exceeding sinfulness of sin: "The good that I would, I do not: but the evil which I would not, that I do. . . . O wretched man that I am! who shall deliver me . . ." (Rom. 7: 19, 24).

Ponder a more modern analogy! In this twentieth century our imaginations are being kindled by the wonderful and fearful consequences of rocket transportation. Here is a rocket with sufficient energy to escape out of the pull of gravity, but with no power left to come back by itself and touch home base. Unless by some miracle the field of gravitation is extended, the rocket will forever circle its original "home" in darkness — lost forever. So it is with man's sinful pride. I have the power to escape out of the pull of the love of God, but my spirit of independence and self-seeking can never of itself take me back within his claiming grace. I haven't got what it takes to get back to God. I have just enough to get away. And it is possible to lose enough of the desire for the fellowship of God to prevent my voluntary and self-induced return to him. I circle vainly in the aimless energy of pride, the ceaseless darkness of despair.

This is the "guilt and power" of sin. I cannot save myself from it. I must *be* saved. If I *am* to be saved, somebody has got to come after me. The field of spiritual gravitation must be extended and claim me again with a power greater than my own. There must be a love that will not let me go. And this is the essential question: In view of my lost and helpless state through sin, does God care enough to come after me — the sinner? The answer is the gospel of our Lord and Savior Jesus Christ. The gravitational field of love is to be endlessly extended at endless cost! Where sin abounds, there does grace much more abound. Long before the inspired fingers of Edwin Markham wrote the familiar verse, the merciful finger of God traced in living flesh His love for you and me. Sinful, rebellious man drew a circle to shut God out. In Christ, God makes triumphant reply:

> "But love and I found the wit to win.
> We drew a circle that took Man in."

This is a belief that matters.

THE STRONG NAME

WHAT's in a name? that which we call a rose By any other name would smell as sweet." Now this is a very beautiful sentiment and, within the romantic setting in which Shakespeare originally put it, a fairly true one. But names do mean something, and there is an inescapable relationship between the right name and the truth it stands for. The most important truth in all our human experience is embodied in a name. When the Word of God was made flesh, a specific name was called for: " And you shall call his name Jesus, for he will save his people from their sins " (Matt. 1:21). The name " Jesus " means " Jehovah is salvation." " God is salvation " because, as we have seen, man's sinful condition is so real, so tragic, so paralyzing in its effect, that only God can do anything about it.

Not far from my home community of Pasadena is the site where several years ago a little girl fell into an abandoned oil drilling. Immediately every resource of the world above her was organized to get down to the place where she lay in utter helplessness, there to rescue her and bring her back up to the realm from which she had fallen. She could not help herself; some power outside herself had to get down where she was and do for her what she could never do alone.

There is another analogy more meaningful to our spiritual situation. It has beeen given words by George Morrison, great Scottish minister of another generation: " The incarnation tells us that if sin is to be grappled with God must come right down into it. I illustrate that from what my eyes have seen among the sick and blind in darkest Africa. If these poor sufferers are to be saved, there must be intervention from a higher realm — from Europe with its science, with its knowledge of the Christian art of healing, with its desire to heal. It is not enough to send them drugs and medicines. Someone from a higher sphere must come among them, carrying in his heart, and head, and hand, the science and skill of the outer world. I have been helped to understand the incarnation by living with doctors in the heart of Africa. If sickness there is ever to be grappled with, some higher being must come into its midst. And if sin is to be grappled with, God must come into its midst. And this we adoringly believe he has done, when, in the person of his beloved Son, he lived our life and died for our sin on Calvary." (*The Ever Open Door;* Richard R. Smith, Inc., 1930.)

The incarnation of the love of God in Jesus Christ underlines and highlights our " lost and helpless state." It reminds us that " all we like sheep have gone astray; we have turned every one to his own way; and the Lord has laid on him the iniquity of us all." Our individual situation is different; but our collective situation is the same! " All . . . have turned . . . every one to his own way." This is the essence of Sin: you are caught in the thicket of pride; I am trapped in the ravine of sinful despair; a third man is struggling in the quicksands of dissolute living; a fourth is just plain lost in a trackless wilderness of complacency, not even knowing he is lost. Our sins are different; our Sin is identical. " All we like sheep have gone astray." And only a *shepherd can* save us.

We cannot find our way back again. We are not even concerned to find our way back again. Only a " *good* shepherd " *will* save us — a very good shepherd: good, because he has skill and courage; good, because he is devoted to the sheep. The incarnation is God's declaration of his eternal willingness to discharge the self-imposed responsibilities of the " Good Shepherd." " The Lord is my shepherd. . . ." God himself is committed to seeking and to saving from everlasting to everlasting that which is lost. " You shall call his name Jesus [God is salvation], for he will save his people from their sins."

" God is salvation " because only the love of God, which is sinned against, can restore the broken relationship. The most insidious quality of Sin is that it keeps man forever from seizing the lost initiative. The only person who can restore the broken relationship is the person against whom I have sinned. I have taken myself out of the relationship; I cannot invite myself back into it. He alone who proposes to maintain the relationship can seek me out, and take my hand in His and impel me to return home once more.

Actually, sinful man is not in the sorry case of the little girl fallen by accident into the abandoned oil drilling, nor is he just a " silly sheep " wandered off without purpose or design. As we have seen in all honesty, the Biblical statement of the nature and character of man's Sin is irrefutable and damning: Sinful man is a son in rebellion; he is a faithless steward found guilty of embezzlement; he has deified his " reason "; he has bowed low to himself repeatedly saying, " I will have no other gods before me! " He can therefore no longer recall his Father's face, nor the way back to his Father's house. He has lost the capacity to think " God's thoughts after him " and therefore he dare not think God's thoughts of forgiving love. He has become a man perverted, undisciplined; he cannot conceive a goodness greater than his own; he has forgotten the meaning of love.

Sinful man has violated a personal relationship to which he was pledged in loyalty and in love. Both because of his proud and rebellious will and by reason of his remorseful and penitent concern, he lives with guilt as the companion of all his ways and days. He can still dream of home, but the dream itself is a condemnation, for he has no business dreaming of that where he should still be, and he knows it. He can dream, but he dare not return, for his Sin stands between him and God.

God has not meant it so; man has made it so! The pride of sin and the guilt of sin in horrible and paradoxical fraternity work together to build a high, bleak, gateless prison wall around man. He has isolated himself from God, and he cannot break through the iron curtain of his own devising. His " reason " cannot help him here, and his conscience is " sharper than a serpent's tooth." God, and God alone, must take the initiative. Only the love despised and rejected can make the saving gesture; only the hands pierced by the nails of man's ingratitude can lift and save; only the feet spiked down to prevent their following after wayward man *can* follow after; only a face smitten and spat upon has the power to turn itself again and yet again toward those who reviled and defiled it. " Jehovah is salvation." " And you shall call his name Jesus, for he will save his people from their sins."

Unless there is a love that will not let me go, I am " a goner "! — past redemption, for I cannot turn my face to God by myself. And I wonder whether the face of God is still such that it can be turned toward me. In a recent junior high communicants class, one of the questions was, " What do you think God is like? " Here is one thirteen-year-old boy's answer to that question: " I would not lie, so I don't know or have a faint idea. I wish he would be a strong-looking person with a small smile on his countenance and a stern but kind pair of eyes." " And the Word became flesh and dwelt among us, full of grace and truth; we have beheld his glory, glory as of the only Son from the Father. . . . No one has ever seen God; the only Son, who is in the bosom of the Father, he has made him known." With Philip we cry, " Show us the Father "! And then we look and behold " the light of the knowledge of the glory of God in the face of Christ " (II Cor. 4: 6). " You shall call his name Jesus [God is salvation], for he will save his people from their sins."

In Jesus Christ, God Almighty, Maker of heaven and earth, Creator of man in His own image, took upon himself the likeness of our sinful humanity, interjected himself into human history, unwilling that sinful man should struggle and die alone and away from his Father's house. On that first Christmas Day so long ago God revealed himself as being " touched with the feeling of our infirmities." He portrays himself forever and from everlasting as " Immanuel: God with us " — with us in all our restlessness and wandering; with us in all our rebellion and our pride; with us in all our failure and resentment; with us in all our sinning. In the incarnation, God breached the wall erected by man's pride and fear and, entering on man's side, there helped him to rediscover the open door back to his Father's house. Is it any wonder the angels sang concerning the incarnation of the love of God, Jesus the Christ, " Glory to God in the highest, and on earth peace among men with whom he is pleased! "?

This is the " peace " that God alone can offer. This is not a peace that I know anything about by myself or within myself. This is not a peace that can ever exist between you and me as sinful men left to ourselves. This is the peace that God alone provides. " So far as I am concerned," God says, " there is peace between your heart and mine." Any man who is still being hard on himself and therefore hard on everybody else, who has failed to be reconciled to himself — as the sinner he is — and therefore remains unreconciled to all the other sinful sons of men, will never come to know " the peace . . . which passes all understanding " until he believes in and appropriates to himself this peace of God. This is not dogmatism; this is reality!

What psychologists are now saying, God Almighty has known and has said for a long, long time. The psychologists are reminding us day after day that the child who feels he is rejected in his own home, even though that feeling of rejection is the legitimate result of his own sin and shortcomings, will grow up inevitably and inescapably to be a problem child. Feeling himself rejected, bereft of parental grace and love and security, he will never grow to be an adult who knows how to give a kindred, reconciling, forgiving love or to receive it from anybody else. This is exactly what God has been trying to get across to us through Jesus Christ, his Son, our Savior, for over two thousands of years.

The incarnation of the love of God in Jesus Christ is God's way of acting out the story of the prodigal son. This story speaks to every human heart. This story is believable because out of some limited experience we have found it to be so: There are fathers good enough, understanding enough, disciplined enough, to forgive their children. We have known fathers after the flesh like that. The all-important question remains, " Is God *that kind* of Father? " And how are we ever to know? We have left our Father's house, and turned our back upon our Father's love. Who are we to dare to say that God still cares and still loves? *Only* by reason of the insight we have found in Jesus, the Christ. The most important point about the parable of the prodigal son is that Jesus told it! And that in speaking *to us,* Jesus speaks *for God.*

Jesus Christ is not just another good man, not just a teacher, not just a preacher who can say what he hopes to be true but who, together with all other sinners, can *only* hope it to be so. "God was in Christ reconciling the world to himself." The incarnation of the love of God in Jesus Christ is an everlasting Christmas card, which bears deeply engraved in the scarred flesh of the Crucified this message: "And now abideth faith, hope, and love; and the greatest of these is love." The name at the bottom of the card is the name that is above every name, the strong name of Jesus — "God is our salvation" — for he has saved his people from their sins! This is a belief that matters.

THE LAMB OF GOD

I T is God, and God alone, who saves from sin. In Paul's wonderful words, " God was in Christ reconciling the world to himself." This is the meaning of the name of " Jesus " — " God is salvation." But there is no salvation without sacrifice; atonement for sin is made only through a costly kind of suffering. Jesus Christ himself was deeply committed to this basic principle of life. Hence the words he used to reinterpret the sacrificial meal he shared with his disciples the night before his death: " This is my body which is broken for you. This is my blood poured out for many for the forgiveness of sins." Jesus evidently thought of himself in the words to which John gave expression when he first laid eyes upon Jesus: " Behold, the Lamb of God, who takes away the sin of the world! " (John 1: 29).

This metaphor immediately takes us back into the earliest pages of the Old Testament. In ancient Israel the highest and holiest sacrifice of all was that sacrifice in which a lamb without spot or blemish, perfect in its physical attributes, was brought before the high altar and there slain, and its pure blood poured out upon the altar of God in atonement for sin.

You and I, in our fancied enlightenment, may look upon

such a blood sacrifice as being primitive in conception and crude in execution, as indeed it was. But we deny at the expense of our own souls the principle involved. There is no salvation without suffering, without sacrifice, without life laid down; if that which is broken and rent asunder is to be mended and brought back together again in a united whole, someone must suffer in order to achieve the reconciliation. Many of us have had difficulty with the searching statement of the Bible, "Without the shedding of blood there is no forgiveness of sins." Some construe this to be the cruel fiat of an implacable and angry Deity. Rather, this is the first principle of innocent and relentless love which wills to forgive at limitless cost to itself. Any analogies from our human experience simply push the cross of Jesus Christ with its burden of suffering love back into the deeper mystery of life. You and I have never suffered so vicariously; even our forgiveness is impure, as is everything else in which we engage. Yet, sinners though we are, we can still apprehend that forgiveness must involve for the love that forgives the kind of vicarious suffering that feels and knows what the forgiven sinner in his ignorance and self-centeredness simply cannot feel and know.

Let me give you one or two very simple examples that will suggest this truth. Many years ago when Mrs. Little and I were setting up housekeeping in Baltimore, Maryland, we numbered among our limited possessions of value a little figurine. It had real value because it was a genuine and a lovely antique. It had great sentimental value because it had been in our family for many years. One day a very fine woman, who was helping to clean our apartment, in carelessness broke that figurine. She said she was sorry, and she *was* sorry, and she was forgiven. But she added a remark that illustrates the truth we are talking about just now. She said: " Don't worry about it; I'll get you another one at the five-and-ten-cent store." You see, part of the burden of suffering in forgiveness is that you not only have to forgive what has been done, and cannot ever be undone, but you also have to forgive the complete lack of apprehension upon the part of the one who has done it as to what has actually happened! The worst part of our Sin is our bland assumption, " It doesn't make very much difference to me; therefore it can't make *that* much difference to God "! And the deepest part of the agony of forgiveness for God is that it makes *all* the difference to him. He suffers because we don't even recognize the magnitude of his suffering.

Let me give you another illustration, which strikes nearer home to the heart of our spiritual situation with God. I once knew a man who made the tragic mistake of giving his wife a perfectly beautiful fur coat by way of making up to her for his disloyalty, which he and she both knew. It did not mitigate her suffering; it intensified it almost beyond endurance. It added to the burden of her suffering love, which was willing to forgive his disloyalty, the recognition that he had not the slightest apprehension of how she was suffering and what it was that he had really violated so far as she was concerned. There cannot be a continuing atonement in a situation like that that does not include the deepest kind of suffering and of sacrifice.

Many of you know and love Sir James Barrie's play *What Every Woman Knows,* and you will remember how Maggie, that loving, faithful little wife, was engaged in forgiving over and over again the disloyalty of a perfectly brilliant, self-centered husband. Finally there came that day when Maggie's brother besought her to give up this self-imposed agony of forgiveness, expostulating, " Maggie, he's not worthy of ye." And she, continuing to suffer as only purity in forgiveness must suffer, replied, simply and quietly, " Ah, you foolish David! " You see, she knew, as David could not then understand, that if atonement is the desired goal, if the broken relationship is ever to be mended and put back together, someone in innocency must agonize and suffer and lay down life. She elected to suffer as she did not need to suffer, but as she must suffer if she insisted upon atonement. She suffered in her husband's unfaithfulness to herself; she suffered in his utter lack of recognition of how and why she suffered. She suffered because she loved him; she suffered because she would save him from himself; and she suffered not in vain! This is the meaning of the cross. And this is the meaning of the words, " Behold, the Lamb of God, who takes away the sin of the world! "

The sensitivity and the purity of the love involved make the suffering in forgiveness the more acute. We are calloused by sin. We accept intolerable relationships every day. We permit the greatest cruelties to be perpetrated and scarcely bat an eye. We become blind to perfectly dreadful situations in human life and lose not a moment's sleep over their continuing existence. God can't, and Christ doesn't! Jesus felt as his " the starving of the poor, the shadow of curse on all, hard words, hard looks, and savage misery, and struggling deaths unpitied and unwept, rich brothers' sad satieties, the weary manner of their lives and deaths that want in love, and lacking love lack all, the heavy sorrow of the world, the horror of the things our brothers bear, the woe of things we make our brothers bear, our brothers and our sisters." (*The Healing Cross,* by Herbert H. Farmer, p. 167. Charles Scribner's Sons, 1939.)

Vicarious suffering involves the agony of continually offering a love that is high and pure and holy, and thus risking its continual rejection and denial. The objects of this high and holy love think such conduct silly and futile; they label its continual proffering of itself " abysmal weakness "; they jeer and scoff at it, spit upon it; they can imagine no greater folly than to be engaged in the business of forgiving until " seventy times seven." Man in his sinful pride stands at the foot of the cross and, looking at his estranged brother, says, " I'd never throw myself at his head," and all the while God in Jesus Christ is throwing himself at man's feet, seeking to stay his willful steps, to make atonement, to effect reconciliation.

In the majestic painting by Holman Hunt, the Christ stands before the closed door of man's heart. " God in Christ " — I remind you of the Pauline phrase — " God in Christ " thus seeks to reconcile the world to himself. God — the Father Almighty, Maker of heaven and earth — who could smash down the barricade and annihilate the sinful, fearful pride which keeps so fast the barred and bolted door — God in Christ divests himself of prestige, prerogative, and pride, and humbly knocks! " Behold, I stand at the door and knock; if any one opens the door, I will come in." Such humility involves eternal suffering upon the part of the God who so stands " in lowly patience waiting." For " lo, that hand is scarred, And thorns Thy brow encircle, And tears Thy face have marred."

You and I, in our pride and in our complete lack of comprehension, say: "Why can't God just announce, ' O. K., I forgive you! '? Why does he have to suffer? It would be a lot easier on him and it would be a lot easier on us if he wouldn't suffer." But *if* he should refuse to suffer, there would be no atonement — no " at-one-ment " — for there would be no high and holy relationship to which to be brought back, since the suffering is symbolic of God's devotion not only to us but to the restoration of the personal relationship he wants to exist between himself and man, his child. God loves me, sinner that I am, but also he loves me as I ought to be, restored and reconciled in him.

Imagine a human father, imperfect and yet a man of high integrity of character and devoted to a wayward child. He purposes to seek his son out amid companions and surroundings of appalling degradation, to which the son has become wholly inured. The father remains dedicated in the very depth of his being to the life his boy has forsaken and rejected; he also remains devoted to the son who bears his name and his own likeness. To such a father, engaged in such a search, the cross is inevitable and inescapable. And for the boy, the way of the cross is the only way back home. For that father to fail to seek out that boy would be to condemn, not to forgive; but for the father simply to say, " O.K., it's all right," would be to condone and not to forgive. Sinful though you and I are, surely we can recognize that a cheap forgiveness does not bring atonement for sin.

One of the greatest stories in the Bible is that of Abraham and Isaac making their painful way up the rugged slopes of Mt. Gerizim, at the top of which Abraham, in a passionate determination to make atonement, to prove to God his willingness to sacrifice to the uttermost, means to offer up his only son. The wood for the fire is strapped upon Isaac's back; the knife is in the father's hand, and the flaming torch which will ignite the burnt offering. Isaac, in his innocency and his ignorance, cries to this father, " My father! . . . where is the lamb for a burnt offering? " Abraham was about to carry out the tragic mistake of believing that sinful man *can* suffer in atonement; his misguided attempt would have been a denial of the reconciling love of God. In agony of mind and perplexity of spirit, he replies to Isaac, " God will provide the lamb, my son." Our Christian faith is that God has so provided!

A Mexican artist, Orozco, once painted the picture of an empty cross and, at the foot of it, the Lord of life and of death, in anger and frustration, standing with ax in hand ready to chop that cross down. Thank God, this is not the true picture of how God feels or what God does. Because God is willing to suffer past our comprehension or belief, there is an atonement which you and I can hope in, and pray for, and sing about: " In the cross of Christ I glory, Towering o'er the wrecks of time; All the light of sacred story Gathers round its head sublime."

We cannot forgive ourselves; we can suffer for our sins, and do, but there is no atonement in that suffering. " Without the shedding of [*innocent*] blood there is no forgiveness of sin." What life is more pure and holy than the life we have sinned against? what love more innocent than the love we have rejected? what blood more redemptive in the purity of its ceaseless flow than the blood our hands have shed? We look with longing for a purity that will sacrifice itself for us, for a love that will stretch itself beside us in our sin and for our sin, and we lift up our eyes and " behold, the Lamb of God, who takes away the sin of the world! " This is a belief that matters.

"THE POWER OF GOD UNTO SALVATION"

THE meaning of anything, according to Aristotle, is disclosed in its final purpose. So the alphabet's true meaning is seen only in the word, in the sentence, in the paragraph, and in the story. The multiplication tables reveal their basic nature in the mathematical formulas with which the physicists describe their universe; the block of marble reveals its true nature in the finished statue; the laws of harmonics come to life in a great symphony; the womb's fishlike embryo in an Abraham Lincoln. You can never understand the true nature of a thing in the beginning; you only understand it in its end result. The completedness of the thing determines its nature. Now this is a basic principle of life, and it applies to the resurrection of Jesus Christ.

Belief in the resurrection is a belief that matters because the resurrection of Christ is the end result which alone gives meaning to our finite existence here and now, in human history, in a world of time and space. (We shall defer for the moment consideration of the implications of the resurrection for what we call the immortality of the individual soul.) For the moment, we look at the resurrection as God's everlasting affirmation that human history has positive, creative, and constructive meaning; that there is a purpose in life

which God proposes to fulfill. " This Jesus God raised up."
(Acts 2: 32.)

There are two fundamental philosophies of history: the
one is " static," the other is " dynamic." The " static " concept of history and of time is held by every aspect of human
thought that remains untouched by the gospel of Jesus Christ
— every single one. The Greeks had a static concept of history and of time. For the Greek, time and history moved in
a circle like a Ferris wheel — the passenger always got off at
the precise point where he got on. The result was a completely negative attitude toward time and all temporal
events. Life was " filled with sound and fury, signifying
nothing." Nothing that ever happens makes any difference
— it all comes out the same. " The music goes round and
round, and it comes out here." It may have had its reveille,
its dance music, but it winds up with taps and a funeral
dirge. In this scheme of things, the individual effort counts
for absolutely nothing so far as affecting the ultimate purpose of life. For life has no ultimate purpose — it isn't going
anywhere. A writer of our own time has reminded us of the
analogy of a magnificent and luxurious ocean liner. It is
equipped with every safety device; it will never sink on the
high seas; its elite passenger list revels in every creature comfort and every pleasurable activity. *But* the vessel isn't going
anywhere! It has no port of call. This whole concept of history and of time Paul sums up in his phrase as " having no
hope and without God in the world."

The other basic philosophy of history and of time is the
Jewish-Christian concept, that there is meaning to time and
to every temporal event because it all goes to fulfill in some
mysterious way past our comprehension God's one increasing purpose. Beginning with the call of Abraham in the
distant shadows of the beginnings of history, and running

right straight through to the last recorded character of time, God has a purpose which God intends to accomplish. Hence the clarion note through the prophet Isaiah: " My word . . . shall not return unto me empty [my creative, dynamic, purpose-filled word], but it shall accomplish that which I purpose."

This whole concept of progress, almost drowned in secularism in our twentieth century, is fundamental to the Christian revelation of the dynamic character of history under the providence of God. What you and I do, then, makes a difference; and what we don't do makes a difference — in our lives, in time and in eternity. This is the meaning of man in history, according to the Bible. God creates man in his own image that man may co-operate with God in bringing an imperfect, unfinished creation to the perfection and the goal for which God has ordained it. That goal includes man's personal fellowship with God and the establishment of a human brotherhood under God — the Kingdom of God on earth. God is committed to realizing this goal, come what may — sin, or death itself. Even man cannot thwart this goal, he cannot reject it, he cannot destroy it. This is the meaning of the resurrection. " This Jesus God raised up."

These are two utterly distinct philosophies of life, of time, and of history — the one spells eternal frustration, the other spells eventual fruition. We might call them " the pin wheel and the rocket " theories of history. Both exhibit lots of activity, both engender that activity by separately packaged units of power. But the pin wheel simply goes endlessly round and round a nail stuck in the barn door; the rocket, in our twentieth century, may eventually reach the moon! So it is with human history. We believe that under the providence of God history will reach its destined goal — but *only* under the providence of God!

Here is the tragedy of our human life. Believing in the rocket theory of history, man finds that history does *not* reach its goal; it falls spent and lifeless to the ground every single time. "Natural" man does not possess the built-in capacity to achieve God's chosen purpose except as he chooses to work at it in fellowship with God. This is the meaning of the fall of Adam and Eve in the allegory of the story of the Garden of Eden. This is the meaning of the curse which God placed upon the ill-conceived attempt by Adam and Eve to divorce the means of progress from a personal commitment to God's purposes in life. Knowledge divorced from faith and fellowship spells disaster. "In the day that you eat of it you shall die." Why? Because of the motivation which will impel you to take into your own hands that which God has reserved for his holy hands, and which you can come to utilize creatively only as you remain in consecrated fellowship with him. Man sets himself up in God's stead and discovers that he does not possess that sufficient modicum of wisdom or of goodness to assist history to realize its God-ordained goal.

Here we must emphasize the Biblical meaning of "death." Death always involves more than physical disintegration. Physical death is in itself bad enough, and for me, as a sinner already spiritually dead, insupportable without God's help. But note the dread phenomenon that all man's "utopias," all man's highest hopes, all man's dreams *die* short of fruition every single time. Man is good enough to hope; he is not good enough to find fulfillment. He can still dream, but he stands in the way of the accomplishment of his dreams. Sinful man knows that every day in every way he isn't getting better and better all by himself, and that his world isn't getting better and better all by itself. It is not the "bad" people who thwart the accomplishment of God's one in-

creasing purpose; it is " good " people who are also sinners
and who agree to disagree about God's purpose and about
their availability to complete that purpose.

Take, for example, one of the most pressing social issues
of our day — segregation. Under the providence of God, according to the love of God revealed in Jesus Christ crucified
on Calvary and risen in power " with healing in his wings "
on Easter Day, the integration of the Negro is an accom-
plished fact, so far as God is concerned. If you think anything different, you need to have your heart examined, my
fellow-Christian sinner. It hasn't happened in history, but,
as surely as Jesus Christ rose from the grave on Easter Day,
it is going to come to pass in this kind of world, in time, and
in history. Now there are only two kinds of people — but
they're not " bad " and " good "; they're all sinners. Some
sinners recognize that God is on the march, and in fear and
trembling and by trial and error, with such light as they have,
are willing to work for the establishment of this next phase
of his Kingdom, and some sinners in fear and trembling are
against it. All we can be sure of is that God, risen in Jesus
Christ, is *on the side* of integration. This is the meaning of
the resurrection of Jesus Christ for the historical process.
" *This Jesus,*" rejected, spit upon, smitten, scoffed at, nailed
upon a cross by the best people of his day, who were scared
to death that if this thing really got loose in the world they
would have to give up and give in and give over and change
their minds and forsake their prejudices and establish a kingdom that " good " people didn't really want — " this Jesus
God raised from the dead! " " This Jesus " has identified
himself with all who aspire and struggle for a larger fellowship, a greater freedom, and God in Christ proposes to complete in time and in history the thing he has set his mind to.

Over and over again, it is the " good " people who disagree

and thwart the purpose of God. Great Britain and the United States, filled with Christians on both sides of the Atlantic, find themselves at cross purposes with regard to the Middle East and the recognition of " Red " China. We are all " good " people. Frenchmen among themselves disagree violently about what to do toward a United Europe or in Algeria. Republicans and Democrats disagree as to what to do about the farm surpluses in a world where many people starve. " Good " people are for and against UNESCO, foreign aid, disarmament. Our frustrations and futility derive from a basic inability to agree on the all-essential first principle: What is God's purpose in history and how are we supposed to implement it? We deny that any purpose not our own could be God's purpose. And if his purpose comes along and tries to pressure us too much, we are perfectly capable of nailing it to a cross if it doesn't suit us.

Is it possible, then, that God's purpose may never reach its chosen goal? that sinful man can and will thwart it every time? that the Savior who comes to rescue the drowning man will himself be gripped in a viselike clutch of death and both sink together into oblivion? Unless God can wrench himself out of the tentacles of man's sinful purposes and establish again his own will for righteousness and brotherhood and peace, history, left to the devices of sinful men, will never accomplish anything. God's refutation of this counsel of despair is the resurrection. " This Jesus God raised up."

The resurrection of Jesus Christ from the dead declares that we will never establish the Kingdom of God by ourselves — this is part of our sin and our pride. It declares that God will establish his Kingdom in his own good time. We can help him if we will; He will do it with somebody's help, whether we will or not. God has entered the stream of his-

tory, and he has come to stay! The risen Christ on the other
side of Easter shouts with a voice that rolls the stars along:
" I shall return! The Kingdom of God is at hand: repent and
believe the gospel! You can crucify God's purpose, you can
stultify his will, you can deny his goal in history, you can
nail the goodness of God to the cross, and every single time
it will come back. It will triumph over sin and death —
whether you like it or not! "

The doctrine of the resurrection is God's promise of revolution: " I will overturn, overturn . . . until he come whose
right it is " to reign. You and I, as followers of Jesus Christ
in this twentieth century, are engaged in a kind of underground movement, filled with internecine warfare, intra-
mural strife — we disagree as to the tactics to be employed,
but, thank God, the strategy is in God's holy hands and he
revealed the strategy on Easter Day. As in the underground
movement in Holland or in Belgium or in the northern part
of France near the close of World War II, we hear that D–
Day has at long last come; the forces of brotherhood and
righteousness and truth have made a beachhead! But will it
be an Omaha Beach where, repulsed with bloody losses, the
purposes of God are repelled? No! The *good* word comes
through that the beachhead is established — it is secure, and
V–Day is therefore made inescapable! There will be many
a Battle of the Bulge, there will be many an Ardennes Forest,
many a crossing of the Rhine, many a repulse, many a bloody
battle fought and lost, but the ultimate victory is determined.
" This Jesus God raised up." This is a belief that matters.

THE VICTORY GOD GIVES

Richard Baxter, an English minister living three hundred years ago, startled his congregation one Sunday morning with the words, " I preach to you this morning as a dying man to dying men." He proved his thesis. He is long since dead, together with every member of his congregation. There is nothing new about the fact of death. But it is startling, when you stop to think about it, and you and I stop to think about it now.

In *The Book of Common Prayer,* in the liturgy for the funeral service, there is a familiar and a searching phrase: " In the midst of life we are in death." This thought-provoking statement was in turn derived from a Latin antiphon composed by Noster, a monk of St. Gaul, in 911, while he was watching workmen build a bridge at Martinsbrook in the peril of their lives. It states the paradox of perplexity and pain: the only completely predictable fact about your life and mine is that we *all* shall die.

Sinful man, unsupported by faith in God and the hope born on Easter Day, can do three things in the face of the fact. First of all, he can refuse to face it. Many and devious and most effective are the ways by which we hide from this fact — or rather, hide this fact from us. Cosmetics skillfully applied either in the beauty parlor or at home can appear to slow down the rate at which we approach death. They do not slacken the death rate at all. The same cosmetics skillfully applied by morticians can gloss over the fact that we have — in fact — died. They will simulate life; they will never stimulate it. A most effective way of hiding from the fact of death is just not to think about it — " out of sight, out of mind." You and I in the twentieth century are embroiled in a veritable cult of ignoring death. It is almost impolite to speak about it in public any more. Nobody ever dies; all " pass on "! This mental maneuver Dr. Samuel Johnson tagged with his usual snort of disdain. His friend Boswell, in praise of living without thought of dying, once said to him, " This, Sir, is great fortitude of mind "; to which Johnson thundered, " No, Sir, stark insensibility."

The wise man at least faces the fact of death. Philip of Macedon was a wise man. Every morning a slave, under his explicit instruction, came into the king's presence and, no matter what he was doing, cried aloud, " Philip, remember that thou must die." We would not value some things in life nearly so much as we do if we remembered that fact more frequently, and we would hold at a much higher premium many other things. The wise man faces the fact of death, but he faces it in utter perplexity, committed to the previously mentioned principle of Aristotle that the ultimate meaning of anything is to be seen in its end results. What can be the meaning of my life which is doomed to end in extinction? The philosopher is completely helpless in the face of his own death. He may hope that his philosophy will live after him, but the philosopher is still going to die. And there is small comfort in George Eliot's pale and wistful hope, " O may I join the choir invisible of those immortal dead who live again in minds made better by their presence!'" Ultimately all the bearers of this racial immortality are themselves going to die. As one commentator has rather realistically observed, "The choir is invisible because it is nonexistent." Death confounds the wisdom of the wise. The life that ends in death is thereby rendered meaningless. The wise man can at least be honest.

The honest man, in turn, faces his death with fear and foreboding — if he's really honest. For the honest man knows that he is not now, and never will be, ready to die. I shall never be prepared to welcome the dark confessor, have him extend to me the scroll of life, hear him say, "Sign here," watch him close the seal and surrender my book of life up to the Judge of life. I do not dare to stand on my record. The honest man knows what Paul was talking about when he wrote, "The sting of death is sin." Only the believing Christian can add with Paul, "But thanks be to God, who gives us the victory through our Lord Jesus Christ" (I Cor. 15:57) — not because we have any power or any merit of our own, but because he loves us with a love that is stronger than our sin, and stronger than our death.

Not the least of the evils of sin is that it has completely colored and betrayed man's concept of what it means to die. "The sting of death *is* sin," but it was not meant to be so. God did not mean that there should be for believing man, related in love to Him, any sting in dying whatsoever. Have you ever thought what would be the reaction of a little unborn babe, still held warm and safe and secure within its mother's body, if it could speculate about its anticipated birth? If that unborn child could reason as you and I — sinful men and women — reason about death colored by our sin, our sense of guilt, our selfishness, the reign of our preposterous ego, that little child would talk like this: "I'm safe and warm and secure right where I am. I have shelter and comfort. All my needs are amply supplied. I have an impersonal and completely satisfying relationship to my mother. I understand that this business of being born is kind of risky. It's even dangerous, I've been told. It involves some pain and no little suffering, and, worst of all, it means that I must give up my present material security, it spells the death of my present relationship to my own mother!" The baby arguing thus would be right on every single count, and tragically, abysmally wrong all the way through from start to finish. His approaching birth is essential to his even remaining alive. If he stays where he is, he *will* die.

Suppose our unborn babe becomes resentful as you and I — sinners — do about the fact of our death. "They tell me that I *have* to be born whether I like it or not! I have no idea what lies ahead. It certainly can't be so good as what I have known. I may never even see my mother again. God simply isn't fair to treat me like this!" Yet every innate capacity for his physical growth, for spiritual development, depends upon that baby's being born, whether he likes it or not! His prenatal relationship to his mother is not to be mentioned in the same breath with the wonder and glory of the relationship that will be his with her on the other side of birth. Do you not see how completely relevant Paul's analogy is? "Now we see in a mirror dimly, but then face to face." So it is with every rich and rewarding relationship in life. This unborn baby's future relationship with his father, with his brothers and sisters, with his future friends, with his future wife, with his own unthought-of children, all await and depend upon his submission to being born. Life the newborn baby has; the life that is abundant awaits him on the other side of birth. And he dares to argue with God his Creator as to whether or not he is willing to be born, *if* he argues the way you and I do about dying!

Death is an inescapable and completely constructive factor in the growth of spiritual life. You don't grow up without dying. You will never be born again unless you die to the life that is partial and inadequate, and, in perfect trust, just as the unborn baby has to do it in perfect trust, submit yourself to the Lord of life who has made physical death a gateway into the life that is abundant. This is part of what Jesus meant when he said, " Whoever would save his life will lose it; and whoever loses his life [who is willing to lay it down, who is willing to submit to the plan and purpose of God for his life] . . . will save it." This is true not only with physical death; this is true of the kind of dying that has to happen to us every day of our lives here and now: going away to school, if you're a youngster, severing the ties with home; father and mother being willing to let the child go away to school and cut the apron strings; getting married, adjusting to marriage, learning to give up to our children as they come along; entering as adults into ever new and larger and untried and less secure relationships and responsibilities as long as we live — never feeling secure because we are never released from the necessity to grow and never released from the necessity to die. Until you and I are willing to become as Jesus Christ was willing to become, in the phrase of Paul, " obedient unto death," we shall never know as he knew the power of the resurrection.

But you and I, sinners that we are, will insist on arguing it out with the Almighty: " I don't like being in this kind of spot. I don't want to grow up this hard and painful way. I am really not enough interested in being better than I am or in knowing something better than I know now to put up with the growing pains of dying and living again. I'll settle for what I possess right now, thank you, Sir." You see, our very concept of death reveals our rebellious state of mind against God. "*I* want to be as God; *I* want to be infinite, eternal, and unchangeable!" God replies: "That is not for the likes of you! You are not going to grow up that way. Newness of life for you must come through dying and being reborn, through death and resurrection." Francis Thompson knew what we are trying to talk about when of his hard-won experience he hears God say:

> "'All which I took from thee I did but take,
>   Not for thy harms
> But just that thou might'st seek it in My arms.
>   All which thy child's mistake
> Fancies is lost, I have stored for thee at home:
>   Rise, clasp My hand, and come!'
>
>   "Halts by me that footfall:
>   Is my gloom, after all,
> Shade of His Rand, outstretched caressingly?
>   'Ah, fondest, blindest, weakest,
>   I am He Whom thou seekest!
> Thou dravest love from thee, who dravest Me.'"

("The Hound of Heaven." The Newman Press. Used by permission.)

"Thanks be to God who *gives* us the victory through our Lord Jesus Christ."

But here is just the trouble — we don't want to take God's hand and come. If being made to lie down in green pastures and being led beside the still waters means that I must walk through the valley of the shadow of death, then, even though God is with me and his rod and his staff will protect me, I insist on saying: "This is wrong, this is unfair, this is tearing me up by the roots from the best that I have known. Nothing can ever be the same again — *I will not have it.*" Far from having faith in God, trusting in his plan for my larger experience of life which involves death, my rebellion against God has taken me out of a personal sense of dependence and trust upon him so that I am now scared to do the very thing that he asks me to do: die.

The penalty of man's sin is *not* his physical death. Adam would have died physically whether he had sinned or not. Death is part and parcel of the newness of life which God has promised spiritual beings. Adam died spiritually because he sinned. " The *soul* that sins shall die." Adam took himself out of relationship to God. He said, " I *will not* die physically," and so he died spiritually. He took himself out of the only relationship that could have enabled him to face his physical death like a man and that could have saved him from the *spiritual* ravages of that physical experience. You and I, without the love of God — the keeping, holding hand of God, stronger than physical death — have no more chance of surviving physical death than a little four-year-old child has a chance of crossing a crowded highway without his father's carrying him. The tragedy of life with four-year-olds, and with eighty-year-olds, and with all of us, is our reiterated assertion of compounded fear and pride, " I will do it by myself," when we neither can nor will. Is it any wonder we are afraid? We have set ourselves to do something God never asked us even to try alone. Having left our Father's house and taken ourselves out of relationship to our Father's love, we are truly lost, and we ought to be afraid.

And then comes Easter! The resurrection is God's demonstration through Jesus Christ raised from the dead that God is stronger than sin or death, and that, while we are going to die physically just as he always meant us to die physically, he is still capable of seeing us through *if* we will stick with him. But he *can't* see us through unless we want him to. Saving faith is committing yourself in trust to the God who brought you into the world whether you liked it or not and is going to take you out of the world whether you like it or not, and believing that in both instances he does it out of love.

In Southern California as in Florida a very adventuresome sport is coming increasingly to the fore. They call it skin diving. There is a basic difference between a skin diver, who does it for fun, and a deep-sea diver, who does it for a living. The skin diver who does it for fun has a couple of tanks of oxygen strapped on his back which enable him to have a pretty good time; he can go down pretty far and stay down pretty long, but, brother, he's got to come back up pretty soon! He doesn't have enough oxygen with him to stay 'way down deep and really do a job! The deep-sea diver, who is called to work under great pressure and at tremendous depth, and often in abysmal darkness, has to have an air hose, which will produce a compensating pressure in his suit which alone will keep him from being squashed into a jelly-like mass. He *knows* that "he hasn't got what it takes" — alone. Before he goes down and every moment while he is in the depths below, he makes sure of his life line and his air hose. He must remain every moment in a "saving" relationship with the inexhaustible supply of oxygen in the world above him — to which he will someday be pulled back up!

You and I are not immortal. That's the Greek idea — that's not the Jewish-Christian idea. God didn't create us immortal. He created us for fellowship with himself, and he said, "If you will stick with me, I'll see you through this life and into the life everlasting." There is no such thing as immortality. My little oxygen tank is going to run out. Jesus Christ came into this world to die upon Calvary's cross and to rise again on Easter morning to remind sinful man that if he is really concerned to live abundantly here and now, and also to bridge the abyss between this life in time and space and the life everlasting, there is only one way of doing it: through a commitment of personal trust in the love of God. Nothing keeps us out of that fellowship except our own unwillingness and our own unbelief; nothing we have done before, no rejection we have previously made, only our present conceit, pride, and fear.

This is the meaning of Easter. There is always a second chance. But until and unless a man embraces that second chance, he has no chance at all of surviving physical death. All any man needs say to God is, " I'm trusting you to see me through." God's answer is the promise of resurrection: " God, who is rich in mercy, out of the great love with which he loved us, even when we were dead through our trespasses, made us alive together with Christ . . . and raised us up with him, and made us sit with him in the heavenly places in Christ Jesus " — if we want it that way. It is given to Christians in a post-Easter world to give thanks in the beautiful and meaningful words of the General Thanksgiving in the *Book of Common Prayer:* " Above all, for thine inestimable love in the redemption of the world by our Lord Jesus Christ; for the means of grace, and for the hope of glory." " Thanks be to God, who gives us the victory through our Lord Jesus Christ." This is a belief that matters.

THE BODY OF CHRIST

Every year I have asked members of our junior high communicants class whether it is necessary for a follower of Jesus Christ to be a member of the church, and every year a great many of these young people say, "No." Before the class is over I hope all of them are willing to change their minds. Any man who is ready to say in his heart and with his lips, "Jesus is Lord," repeating the earliest formulary of the Christian church, is making a commitment of faith in a fellowship with God through Jesus Christ which will inevitably involve him in a fellowship of faith and life with other Christians. To believe in "this Jesus," the Spirit of God incarnate, the reconciling power of God's love made flesh, the demonstration of redemptive grace on Calvary, the power of God unto salvation through the resurrection, is to believe in the necessity of identification with the church, the body of Christ on earth. This is so because of the nature of the church. The church is a fellowship of reconciliation composed of other weak, sinful, vacillating, forgiven and forgiving men and women, like you and me, through whom the unifying Holy Spirit of God provides a continuing demonstration center of the power of God's love. In the church, the love of God still incarnate in *sinful* flesh reaches out to attract other lives in need of a fellowship of forgiveness and so to extend the Kingdom of God on earth. Paul properly wrote of and to the church, " You are the body of Christ, and every one members individually " (I Cor. 12: 27). This is a belief that matters.

First of all, Christ is the Head of the true church, and this true church is utterly different and distinct from any other group of men and women on the face of the earth. There are many fine fellowship and service organizations in which we take pride, of which we may be members: but Christ is not the head of Rotary; he is not the head of Kiwanis; he is not the head of the Order of Masons or of the Knights of Columbus; he is not the head of the United States, or of the United Nations; he is not the head of the National Associa-tion of Manufacturers or of the combined organization of the CIO and AFL. All these organizations of men are com-mitted to worthy purposes, to advancing a limited fellow-ship, but all are utterly incapable of promoting the kind of reconciliation that the Spirit of God alone, regnant in the hearts and minds of men and women, can provide. Christ is the Head of *his church*.

Now from this belief there stem two important corollaries. First of all, the true church of which Christ is the Head is in-visible. It does not follow that because a man joins a local church he has joined the church of which Christ is the Head. That depends upon the inner commitment of his own mind and heart, which only Christ knows. As Saint Augustine once wrote, " There are many sheep without and many wolves within." The true church known to Christ alone could embody men and women who, for one or another reason understandable to God alone, remain outside a visible church organization and yet are still completely animated by the reconciling power of the love of God; and there can be men and women and young people who are members of a visible church who have not yet really committed themselves to the forgiving love of God which will reconcile them to him, to their own sinful selves, and to their brothers, whom it is not always easy to love, to understand, and to forgive.

There is a second corollary stemming from this important truth. If Christ is the Head of the church, then the church, to be truly the church, must first of all address itself to discerning what is the mind of Christ and to submitting itself in obedience to " this Jesus " whom God raised up, who is still committed to a sacrificial, painful kind of redemption and of reconciliation to this world. The task of the church as the body of Christ is the same task that confronted Jesus in his own human body. The church must become, in the first instance, " obedient unto death, even death on a cross." The church has no other function or purpose in this world than to demonstrate the reconciling power of the love of God within its own body and through its body in the world of men lost and afraid. John Baillie, in *Invitation to Pilgrimage* (Charles Scribner's Sons, 1942), truly wrote, " The church is a divine society created by God himself, a society to which men are elected, not by any human vote but by the grace of God, a society whose one condition of membership is faith in God's forgiving love." The true church is " the body of *Christ,*" a fellowship of forgiveness, committed to the gospel of reconciliation in this kind of world at cost to itself.

" *You* are the *body* of Christ." On the other hand, there is a visible body, and we are it! Can this possibly be true? Dr. J. S. Whale, of England, has stated in breath-taking words, " This is why the visible church is rightly known by all Christians as an extension of the incarnation " (*Christian Doctrine,* p. 140; Cambridge University Press, 1941; used by permission). But this is an appalling thought! After we look at Jesus Christ, dare we add, "*Now — we* are his body?" This is indeed coming down from the Mount of Transfiguration, where we have seen the glory of God revealed in the face of his only begotten Son, only to find ourselves confronted with an epileptic boy who cannot even control his own actions upon occasion. Can we believe of such as ourselves the promise that says, "You are now become the instrumentality of the reconciling Spirit of God in this kind of world"?

This *is* " the power of God for salvation "! *We* are the *body* of Christ? weak, vacillating, proud and prejudiced, filled with frustrations and fears within, fightings without, scarcely able to command our own loyalties for twenty-four hours at a stretch? We sing, "Like a *mighty army* moves the church of God," but in all honesty the title of one of Kenneth Roberts' historical novels best describes us, *Rabble in Arms.* So we appear to ourselves and to the world — but not to God in Jesus Christ! Such is the grace of God that he still humbles himself, he still takes upon himself the guise of a servant, he is still found in the likeness of sinful men, he still stoops to conquer, he permits his reconciling Spirit to be clothed with the church. " You are the *body* of Christ."

Paul's tremendous declaration implies, "Don't sell the church short." " O where are kings and empires now Of old that went and came? But, Lord, thy church is praying *yet*." Weak, frail, helpless, divided against itself, it still prays for the promise of God in Jesus Christ to be fulfilled in its broken body. Through its all-too-human fellowship in our day and time something of the reconciling, redeeming, changing, power-laden Spirit of God will still get hold of men and women such as ourselves, and make a difference in us, and through us in this world. And this *is* what has happened. There is no political, economic, social institution of Jesus' time that has not long since been swept into the dust heaps of yesterday. This inadequate instrument of the power of God, the church, is still living and working and praying and serving.

How did this miracle ever come about? Well, surely not by our own unaided help. We are the body of Christ, and "the performing God" accomplishes his purpose *through* the likes of you and of me! We assume that our pseudo-Christian civilization is still kept going by some kind of sociological osmosis. This is not so. It is kept going by the church of Jesus Christ (not the visible church only) on earth, "praying yet," preaching the Word of God to every generation, communicating through dedicated Christian fathers and mothers to the children of the next generation the gospel of Jesus Christ, still infusing every personal and social relationship of the world of our day and time with the grace of forgiveness, by which alone man lives, albeit haltingly, falteringly, and thus saving the world in every generation again and yet again.

"You are the *body* of Christ." The church can say in some very real measure, as Jesus said of himself at the outset of his earthly ministry: " The Spirit of the Lord is upon me, because he has anointed me to preach good news to the poor. He has sent me to proclaim release to the captives and recovering of sight to the blind, to set at liberty those who are oppressed, to proclaim the acceptable year of the Lord." Yes, the church is the visible body of Christ on earth, a bruised and broken body, sometimes almost a deformed body, bearing alike the scars of sacrifice and the stigmata of its own sin, but still used and blessed of God, still the body of Christ ministering to the necessities of the saints, who are at one and the same time sinners. And there is no gospel of reconciliation preached, demonstrated, or applied apart from the working of the Spirit of God in his body upon this earth.

The plural pronoun in Paul's assertion is of utmost importance: "You are the body of Christ." The text is clarified by the use of the archaic "Ye" in the King James Version. "Ye [it is plural] are the body of Christ." *I*, alone and unaided, am not the body of Christ. Not one of us, alone and by himself, could ever become the body of Christ, but *together* "we are the body of Christ." Now this is more than just the old shibboleth that has come down in American history, "In union there is strength." This reminds us that the Spirit of God is not promised to the individual; it is promised to the "beloved community," who together seek to discern the will of God and to embody the Spirit of the risen Christ.

One of the great heresies to which the Christian church becomes prone over and over again permits the individual Christian to go off on a tear all by himself and say, "I have now got the guidance of God for what he wants me to do." The guidance of God and the grace of God and the mind of Christ and the reconciling power of the love of God are promised to the church — to the organism, to the collectivity of minds who agree as to their need to be forgiven and who are dedicated to a co-operative search for the power to be reconciled to one another and to all men. The early Christian church was a miraculous demonstration of the power of the risen Christ after the resurrection. It was a resurrection organism. Immediately the Jew who had become a follower of Jesus Christ and the pagan Gentile who had become a follower of Jesus Christ, who, up to the moment of their conversion, had been at swords' points through the centuries, found themselves worshiping hand in hand and heart with heart before the same God, imbued with the same power of the same reconciling love.

The power of Pentecost was the demonstration of the ability of the Holy Spirit to bring and to keep sinful men in a fellowship of grace which transcended all their " natural " prejudices and predilections. We have no problems, no issues, no confrontations of divisions and vicissitudes in the desperate circumstances of our twentieth century that did not confront the early Christian church. Whether it is the integration of the Negro or whether it is the achievement of an increasing measure of peace on earth, good will among the nations of mankind, there is still no power for salvation except a demonstration of the ability of the grace of God in and through the church to transcend all the man-made barriers of pride and fear. And this world is not going to be saved in this twentieth century except as we who are the body of Christ on earth today lay hold upon the ancient power that enabled the body of Christ in the first century to demonstrate before the world that in Christ there is neither Jew nor Greek, slave nor free, male nor female, white or colored, ruler or ruled, but all are one in Christ Jesus. No other organization is going to step forward with that demonstration of power — not Kiwanis, not Rotary, not the United States of America, not the United Nations, certainly not the National Association of Manufacturers, or organized labor, because none of them are sufficiently submissive, obedient unto death, to the Spirit of God revealed in Jesus Christ and promised to his church.

None of us by ourselves are adequate to assume this high and holy obligation because we too are still sinners. But the grace of God is upon the church. Christ says: " I know you are not adequate. I promise you the reconciling presence of the Spirit of God, by which alone you will become adequate. *You* are the body of Christ and every one members individually." *You* have accepted certain obligations; you have committed yourselves to certain inexorable, unalterable truths. You claim participation in a beloved community, in a reconciling fellowship. You are now charged with a demonstration of the reconciling love of God. "This Jesus," incarnate, crucified, triumphant, ascended to heaven and sitting on the right hand of the throne of God, now delivers to you the keys of the Kingdom, the reconciling power of the Holy Spirit. Here is the relevance of the great confession Simon Peter made at Caesarea Philippi. Jesus said, "What are men saying about me?" The disciples replied, "Oh, men all agree that you are a great prophet, you're a great preacher, you're a good man — why, you're the best man the world has ever seen!" None of that was satisfactory to Jesus Christ. He kept pressing, "But whom say *ye* that I am?", and finally Simon Peter confessed, "Thou art the Christ. . . ," the reconciling demonstration of the power of God. And Jesus rejoiced, "Give me enough men and women like you and 'upon this rock [of personal, faithful commitment] I will build my church; and the gates of hell shall not prevail against it'" (Matt. 16: 13–16). "*Now, you* are this body of Christ and individually members of it." This is a belief that matters.

THE MEANS OF GRACE

L ATE one night Jesus of Nazareth had a visitor — a man of deep piety and of exemplary life, sincerely thoughtful and as sincerely perplexed. He came seeking to find out how a man grows up spiritually. And before he had uttered a complete sentence to state his desire, Jesus told him flatly: " Ye must be born again."

A man has to be born again because he was born in the first place into a deep dependency. He is dependent upon love: he has to receive it; he has to give it. A man who is not beloved and who does not know how to give love is not a man. He was created by and for love. Man's sin is that he does not believe that this is so. He wants to be independent. He likes to believe he needs neither to be loved nor to love. He thinks he can " live alone and like it "! And so he has to be born a second time; he has to die to his selfish feeling of independence and be born again into the kingdom of dependency upon love. He has to find out somewhere along the line that he will never grow up spiritually until he discovers how to receive love and to pass along a kindred understanding, forgiving, reconciling love to others. This has to happen to a man at least once in a big way; but it does not happen only once; it happens again and again and yet again. There is a reiterated crucifixion of the "old man" and his spirit of vaunted pride and independence; there is a reiterated resurrection into the Kingdom of God. He must be born again and yet again into a sense of dependence upon the forgiveness God's love alone provides. This is a belief that matters.

How does this happen? Even in the realm of the spirit there are means to the attainment of certain ends. Bricks are not made without straw. There are means of grace, and chief among the means of grace is the Word of God. As J. S. Whale has properly expressed it, "Saving faith comes to men not through any intellectual gymnastics; it is wrought by the Holy Spirit of God in the heart through the preaching of the gospel" (*op. cit.,* p. 152). Peter truly expresses it in one of his letters: We are "born again . . . by the word of God, which liveth and abideth for ever" (I Peter 1:23).

Does it seem strange to believe that the Word of God can work such a transformation? Consider, then, for a moment the power of any "word" to create or to destroy. As children we prattled, "Sticks and stones may break my bones, but words will never hurt me." This is a lie. Words have ultimate power of spiritual life and death. Men and women walk up and down the byways of our common life, hurt almost beyond redemption because they cannot forget words of rejection, of cynicism, of resentment, of anger, and of hatred. And no one of us walks with head erect save as we are supported by some word of reconciliation and redemption and forgiveness from someone in some relationship thus saved or restored by the word of grace. Every word has such power in every meaningful human relationship.

I remember during the Korean War a live television broadcast from Korea under the auspices of — who else? — Edward R. Murrow. A group of Greek soldiers were answering

27840

" mail call." I didn't need to understand their words; I saw
their souls being restored by " good news from the far country " of home — the word that said to them, " We still love
you, we still think of you, we still care about you; sundered
by miles of space, we still walk with you in your valley of the
shadow of death."

One of the greatest accolades ever given in Scripture was
awarded to Job by his friends, who otherwise weren't of
much comfort to him. They said to him, " Your words have
kept men on their feet! " How true that is! So the Word of
God revealed in Jesus Christ has enabled spiritual paralytics
to rise, take up their beds, and walk again because their souls
were restored; they experienced alike a crucifixion of the old
man and a resurrection of the new man in hope and joy and
courage and faith.

The human heart was made the way it is in the first instance by the creative, restoring Word of God: " In the beginning was the Word, and the Word was with God, and the
Word was God. He was in the beginning with God; all
things were made through him, and without him was not
anything made that was made." (John 1: 1–3.) And God
through his creative Word declared, " I will make man in
my own image with a deep, abiding hunger and thirst for
the word of reconciliation and restoration which it will be
my grace to speak and his capacity to hear and apprehend,
and live by."

Long, long ago the Word came to Abraham, saying, " Go
from your country and your kindred and your father's house
to the land that I will show you " (Gen. 12: 1). And there
and then began, in the dim, far-off shadows of human history, a pilgrimage that did not end until Abraham's spiritual
children found in Jesus Christ, the " Word . . . made
flesh," the end of all their spiritual being. Ever since, men

and women have looked at him and said with his own first
disciples: " Lord, to whom shall we go? You have the words
of eternal life " (John 6: 66).

The chief responsibility of the church, the body of Christ
on earth, is to communicate to men and women and young
people this means of grace, the preaching of the Word of
God. " How are they to believe in him of whom they have
never heard? And how are they to hear without a preacher?
And how can men preach unless they are sent? As it is written, ' How beautiful are the feet of those who preach good
news! ' " (Rom. 10: 14–15.) Out of this passage and others
kindred to it in our New Testament was born the Protestant
Reformation, with its recovery of emphasis on the preaching
of the Word of God. When you walk into a Protestant
church, you no longer see the altar as the focal point, the
altar before which, through the centuries, men and women
sought to appease a God whose sacrificial love they could not
know or dare to assume. The altar is replaced by the pulpit
and the lectern, the written Word and the preached Word
of God, for this God has now come into our human history
and through the cross upon our Communion table has declared to us the reconciling word of fellowship, forgiveness,
understanding, and redemption.

Evelyn Underhill does not put it too strongly: " The center of all is now the constant proclamation of the Word, the
vehicle of God's self-disclosure to men. The Word is, for
evangelical worship, something as objective, holy, and given
as the blessed sacrament is for Roman Catholic worship. Indeed, it is a sacrament — the sensible garment in which the
suprasensible Presence is clothed. Preaching of this category
is to be classed as a supranatural act, bringing all those who
submit themselves to its influence into communion with
God." Such is the means of grace toward rebirth, the restora-

tion, the resurrection of the human soul.

This means that there is a vast difference between a sermon and a lecture, and there is a vast difference between a man who is preaching and a man who is lecturing. The lecturer properly addresses himself to the minds of men. Dr. Whale states eloquently, " The gospel is not a book but a living Word, which God himself cries aloud to all the world, using as his mouthpiece those whom he calls his ministers." " 'God's Word,' said John Calvin, ' is uttered by men like ourselves; common men who may even be much inferior to us in dignity and social importance. But when some insignificant little man is raised up out of the dust to speak God's Word, he is God's own minister, God's very lieutenant. The preaching of the Word of God is the Word of God. Thus the preacher of the Word is more than a historian. He is a herald! He is no mere lecturer stimulating interest in the past, but an evangelist whose vocation and responsibility it is to cry, " This day is this scripture fulfilled in your ears — now is the accepted time." The herald is not sent to deliver his own soul, but to preach the glorious gospel of the blessed God. He is a King's messenger, no more and no less. The vitality of his message does not depend upon him, nor upon his character; he may be a bad man. Nevertheless, says Saint Paul, Christ is preached. All Christian preaching finds its only sanction and power in the authority of a human life, death, and resurrection through which God spoke in the fullness of time, and through which, by his Spirit in the church, his body, he speaks so long as time endures.' " (Whale, *op. cit.,* pp. 153–154.) This is a belief that matters.

This means that the preacher is nothing; but that the preaching of the Word is essential. There is a danger here, however. In the Protestant Church there tends to be an over-emphasis upon the preacher rather than upon the Word being preached. How many times have you heard people say, " I went to hear Buttrick today," or, " I tuned in on Sockman this morning "! Paul wrote the proper footnote to that question: "What then is Apollos? What is Paul? Servants through whom ye believed, as the Lord assigned to each." Preachers may come and preachers may go, but the Word of God abides and lives forever. How many times do people say, "Who's preaching today?", before they will decide whether or not they propose to submit themselves to the preaching of the Word of God! What difference does it make who is preaching today — the Word of God is being preached!

A B–52 bomber crashes in flames and some of the crew are saved and some are lost. Anguished parents across the country who had boys stationed at the air field from which that plane took off wonder whether any of their boys are on that plane; they wonder whether, if their boys were on that plane, they were among those whose lives were saved. Finally, to some, comes a rejoicing telegram, " I am safe! " Does it make any difference which particular Western Union messenger boy carries that message to the front door? We are reborn in hope by the hearing of the Word of God which lives and abides forever. Men and women are not born again by listening to Elijah or one of the prophets, but by giving heed to the proclamation of the Word of God made flesh.

The hearing of this Word of God — church attendance, church worship — is a spiritual essential in life. Men like to talk about communing with God in nature. God is in nature; he speaks through nature; but the most important things God has to say to the human heart — the things my heart must hear or die — *God does not say through nature!* " The voice that rolls the stars along speaks all the promises," but he doesn't speak them through the stars! He speaks them through the Word of God made flesh. So, too, we properly praise " music, the universal language of the soul." But a man is not saved within the depths of his soul by listening to great music. Saul of old found temporary relief from his soul sickness through music struck by skillful hands from David's lovely harp, but Saul ultimately plunged his sword into his own flesh because he would not listen to the word of God. What does it profit a man if he gain the whole world [of music, of art, of nature, of philosophy] and lose his own soul? The battle for personal purity, the life of stewardship, the understanding of God's will for us in the face of the crushing social and international issues which press upon us in this twentieth century — these will never be won, embraced, or achieved apart from the enabling Word of God. This saving Word is preached only in the church — the repository of this means of grace, the place of the restoration of the soul, where we are born again by " the word of God, which liveth and abideth for ever."

Thank God, this Word does live and it does abide forever! In an upper room of long ago, in the catacomb, in the Gothic cathedral, in the Nonconformist chapel, around a jeep in Korea, in a thatched hut in deepest Africa, from " Greenland's icy mountains " to " India's coral strand " — the Word of God is preached in all ages and in every tongue. In every dialect and with varied emphasis, colored inevitably by the mind and heart and experience of the messenger, conditioned by his mental and spiritual capacity — the Word is *forever* " the power of God for salvation " *wherever* it is heard and believed. Still on the first day of every week Christ rises again from the dead in the preaching of his Word: still the Spirit and power descend at Pentecost, renewing, revitalizing, confirming and strengthening the beleaguered souls of men. This Word, seemingly so frail, so inadequate, so helpless, has miraculous staying powers.

Paul knew and wrote about " the foolishness of preaching." Any preacher worthy of his salt wonders about " the foolishness of preaching." But history demonstrates that it is stronger than any two-edged sword. Almost twenty centuries ago, according to legend or to history, a man named Peter was fleeing Rome and the Word of God came to him along the Appian Way, asking quietly, insistently, " *Quo vadis?* " " Whither goest thou? " Armed only with that Word, Peter " reversed his field " and went back to Rome, there to preach the living Word at the cost of his own life. Centuries later the Word of God came to one Martin Luther, enabling him to say, " Here I stand; God helping me, I can do none other." His face set like a flint against prince and prelate alike, the kingdoms of this world arrayed against him, this one man, armed only with the rediscovered Word of God, sounded a tocsin which became the Protestant Reformation. In our crucial day, Dibelius, servant of God, writing from a prison cell under the Nazi regime, quotes almost word for word an earlier word of Paul from a much earlier Roman cell: " Wherein I suffer trouble, as an evildoer even unto bonds; but the word of God *is not bound!* " A Dietrich Bonhoeffer and a Cardinal Mindszenty bear kindred and courageous testimony to this eternal truth. Herein lies the power of the church, the body of Christ on earth; to it is committed the communication of the means of grace, the preaching of the Word of God.

It may be a little handful of men and women in this mission or on that street corner, in a prayer meeting or in a crowded stadium — numerically speaking, the hearers of the Word are a minuscule, pitiful human segment of the world of our day. Yet here is the hiding of power: wherever the Word of God is preached, heard, and embraced, there follows the salvation of the souls of men and the overturning of kingdoms of this world! A young man by the name of Grenfell stops in at a mission in London, the Word is preached, the invitation is given, and Grenfell stands, partly because nobody else is standing up and he doesn't like to see the preacher embarrassed by such a pitiful response to his challenge — and Labrador is saved by the preaching and the healing ministering of this young man. A minister in a lonely Scottish church is asked to resign by his session because in the preceding year only one lad joined the church; but that one little boy turns out to be Robert Moffatt, who opens up the entire continent of darkest Africa to the preaching of the Word of God and the Kingdom of Jesus Christ on earth. Another minister in a little town in the upper tier of counties in western New York State writes in a moment of despair in his diary about the lack of vitality in his church — only one *young* couple received into membership in twelve months and they are moving away! But that young couple happen to be Marcus Whitman and his bride, who move out to our great Pacific Northwest and save it through the preaching of the Word for God and country!

"The Word of God . . . liveth and abideth for ever" through a kind of spiritual chain reaction. One of the hallmarks of the true church, which is the body of Christ on earth, is the capacity to reproduce within its own spiritual fellowship young people who become dedicated in their own lives to the preaching of this gospel of Jesus Christ. Another hallmark of the true church is a growing capacity to produce a genuine "priesthood of all believers" in which mutual understanding, forbearance, and acceptance facilitate the sealing of the Word of grace to the hearts of those inside and outside the visible church. A word of real understanding, spoken without any pretension of " professionalism " or the use of " pat " pious phrases, but spoken by a layman in a real endeavor to communicate concern, can prove to be the Word of grace by which men are born again.

Walt Whitman once wrote, " Music is what wakens in a person when the instruments revive him," and newness of spiritual life is what wakens in the human soul when the instrument of God's grace revives it. The primary means of grace is the preaching of the Word. " The Spirit and the Bride say, ' Come.' And let him who hears say, ' Come.' And let him who is thirsty come, let him who desires take the water of life without price." (Rev. 22: 17.) Such is the living and abiding Word of God by which we are born anew. This is a belief that matters.

LOVE AND SACRAMENT

O NE of life's mysterious truths is this: In the final analysis,
love can never communicate itself adequately through
words; it must resort to action. Words become like the fuses
in the switch box. When the load gets above a certain point,
they simply fizzle and burn out. They cannot carry the load
of love and grace. So love, in order to convey its fullest meaning, always must fall back upon "sacrament." Sacrament is
the dramatization — the acting out — of the love that will
not let us go.

Moreover, the acts of love remain longer in the memory,
and remain there with more compelling force, than do the
words of love. For instance, in thinking back upon my
mother's love and devotion to her home, her children — and
her God — I do not think in terms of what she said so much
as in terms of what she did. (I may have a visual memory
rather than an audial one.) At any rate, I recall many simple
things she did: I see her baking certain delectable cinnamon
rolls in a wood stove; I remember her reading to us from
Charles Dickens by a kerosene lamp in our living room; I
visualize her darning seemingly inexhaustible heaps of stock-
ings by that same lamp. More meaningful still, I remember
her singing, "He leadeth me: O blessed thought" and

" Jesus, Savior, pilot me " in the middle of wakeful, fever-
filled nights through the course of a prolonged bout with the
1918 " flu." Most particularly, I can see her now in the pew
beside her children, lifting a very tight-fitting veil in order
to partake of the elements of the Lord's Supper. I vividly remember these little " sacraments " of the home — actions of
hers which now in recollection enforce upon me still the
relationships and values she held dear.

Action and remembered action are powerful means of
conveying powerful and motivating emotions. Hence, we
" leap " for joy! We can't put it all into words; we have to
get up and move around. We " tremble " and " run " for
fear. We embrace for love. We cook a meal, drive a car, or
do any little thing for our friends in sorrow — thus seeking
to put into some kind of action the comfort of friendship
which cannot be contained in words alone. Goethe hit the
nail right on the head: " The highest cannot be spoken; it
can only be acted." So God came to us in Jesus Christ, the
Word made flesh, the Word in action. So too Jesus Christ
resorted to " sacraments," certain acted-out things, in order
to convey to us the wonderful love of God. And when we do
them " in remembrance " of him, they help us to recall the
love that will not let us go.

The sacraments of the church, in our Protestant conception of them, are two in number because they are those things
which were given to us by Christ himself, in which he participated, in which he asked us to participate. Long before
the church formulated a liturgy, long before there were rules
and regulations and church councils defining accepted modes
of procedure, long before there was an ordained clergy, the
first Christians — from the very beginning — " received his
word, *were baptized,* and . . . devoted themselves to the
apostles' teaching and fellowship, to the *breaking of bread*

and the prayers " (Acts 2: 42).

The sacraments, as well as the preaching of the Word, are " means of grace." That is, the sacraments not only stand for something precious in the past, they give effect in our souls to something in the present, something that is unseen but eternal. This is true of all valid symbols.

Three summers ago we were privileged to visit Great Britain. We did all the wonderful things all American tourists do! Among other visits, we went to the Tower of London and saw the breath-taking collection of the crown jewels. (You look at them and you do not really believe it is so!) Most of the time these fabulously valuable jewels are kept under lock and key and the strict supervision of an armed guard, but once in a great while they come out. Why? They become symbols of the unity, integrity, loyalty, and strength of the British Commonwealth of Nations. Within recent memory the crown, the orb, and the scepter were placed upon the casket in which reposed the body of a great and beloved king. A few months later the crown rested upon the head, and the orb and scepter were grasped by the hands, of a new and gracious sovereign, Queen Elizabeth II. So employed, they serve a very different purpose from that of simply being exposed to the openmouthed amazement of the casual tourist; they not only remind, but they convey to the hearts of loyal men and women that which is unseen but eternal — the stuff of which the very warp and woof of life is made — unity, strength, sacrificial commitment, love.

The same thing happens when a bride and groom stand before the minister at the point in the wedding ceremony when the ring is given and received. The ring is a symbol, a token. It not only stands for something; it conveys what it stands for to the believing heart! " This ring I give thee in token and pledge of our constant faith and abiding love."

The ring is not essential to either the legality or the reality of the marriage vows, but it does confirm and seal and add something important. For we creatures of time and space, of flesh and blood, are helped by the transference from hand to hand of a tangibility which in turn represents the communion of heart with heart. Love communicates itself by token and through sacrament.

So it is with the sacrament of the Lord's Supper when celebrated in and by the church, the believing body of Christ. It is something like playing the score of Beethoven's Fifth Symphony: every time the score is played, the soul-moving music swells again into the hearkening ear and wells up again within the longing heart of the hearer.

Here we confront a point of great and vital difference between our Protestant conviction and that of our Roman Catholic friends. We do not believe, as Protestants, that in the sacrament of the Lord's Supper, for instance, Jesus Christ literally offers himself up again in saving love. There is no moment in our celebration of this sacrament when, by an authoritative spoken word, the elements of bread and wine actually change into the body and blood of Christ. We do believe that this sacrament conveys to us the eternal love of the eternal Christ, who is present with us whenever together *as a company of believers* we lay our hands upon things seen in order that his unseen hands may be laid upon our renewed and rededicated lives.

One of the important things about a sacrament is what it means to the person who created and established it in the first place. "This do in remembrance of me." The sacrament reminds us that it means something to God in Christ! Therefore it means everything to us. Again referring to the wedding ring, if ever there comes a time between a husband and his wife when the ring he once gave her no longer repre-

sents to him a pledge of loyalty and love, then at that moment the meaning of the ring changes for her — it cannot but be so. The sacraments of God's love — Baptism and the Lord's Supper — hold eternal meaning for the men and women who receive them in faith because these sacraments represent the everlasting love of God. " This do in remembrance of me." The one who speaks " is the same yesterday and today and for ever."

Furthermore, the sacraments speak for themselves; they are not dependent upon some kind of mysterious, magical power possessed by the man who administers them. This is of the utmost importance for faith. In the Protestant Church of the so-called " evangelical " tradition we have ministers to baptize children and adults and help us to celebrate " Communion," in order that things may be done in decency and in order in the church down through the generations of men. But the minister himself conveys nothing that is efficacious or saving by virtue of any peculiar power *he* possesses. The sacrament speaks for itself.

I remember my father's telling a story that illustrates this point. Many years ago, my grandfather was superintendent for home missions in the Presbyterian Church U.S.A. for the State of Texas. In those days the only way of getting from church to church, or from home to home, was either on horseback or in a buckboard behind a span of horses. Travel took time! Word came to my grandfather one day that in an isolated home 'way in the back country there was a little baby desperately ill. The distraught parents wanted Dr. Little to come as quickly as possible to baptize their child. Grandfather saddled his horse, and away he went across the prairies. But the miles were too long and the horse too slow; the little baby died before the minister arrived. The grief-stricken mother greeted my grandfather at the door, and the

first question she asked was this: " When I knew you were not going to get here in time, I poured a little water into the washbasin and baptized our baby myself — was this all right? " " Of course," my grandfather replied instantly; " it doesn't take anybody special to perform the sacrament when man's faith and God's love are both present! "

This brings up another important emphasis: The sacrament becomes truly a means of grace in proportion as it is received in faith. There is nothing magical about it. It must be believed to represent and to convey the love of God, or else it remains an empty gesture. Once more the wedding ring comes to our aid! If the bride does not believe that her groom loves her, the wedding ring isn't going to mean anything to her, regardless of how much it means to him. So it is with the sacraments. All we can do — but this is what we must do — is to accept the love as offered, the grace as given *and* the validity of the means by which this love and grace are dramatized as being sufficient for our abiding human need for such love and grace. Our souls are fed by the bread of forgiveness; our hearts are cleansed by the water of life. There is nothing automatic about grace. Here again we disagree with our Roman Catholic friends. The sacrament of the Lord's Supper is not like a blood transfusion: Baptism is not like " taking a shot "! A transfusion or an injection of aureomycin will presumably help a man even though he is unconscious at the time of administration. This is not true of the sacraments — at least Protestants do not so believe. The grace of God is received by the understanding, appropriating heart.

This contention in turn raises a very real problem for all sincere " believers " who are honest enough to realize the littleness of their faith upon many an occasion. For we must admit: " But I don't always believe as I should or as I want

to when I participate in the sacraments. On any given Sunday morning when I come to church and I find the elements spread upon the Communion table, I must confess — if I am absolutely honest — I just am not in the mood today! The whole thing leaves me cold; it doesn't reach down and get hold of me where I live and struggle and suffer." What a completely natural and human state of mind! But this is just why we celebrate the sacraments *in the church* (not in the church building!). For who does the believing? The church does the believing — the church of all ages — the church militant — the church triumphant!

This is the marvel and the mystery of the sustaining fellowship of faith to be found in the " body of Christ," the " beloved community," " the church of the living God," the body of believers. There are days when my personal faith is entirely insufficient. All I could possibly do would be to echo the father of the epileptic boy when he was confronted by Jesus with a demand for faith before help could be applied: " Lord, I believe; help thou mine unbelief." Then it is the church, the body of believers, that undergirds my feeble, faltering faith with its triumphant, abiding faith and hope and love! So, when we baptize our children, we baptize them in the presence of the church. The church joins the vitality of its faith to the faith of the parents. So only is there provided a sustaining, comforting, uplifting, dynamic power of faith through all the ages, insuring the communication of saving faith to each successive generation.

This is a principle of the widest application. No man walks alone, adequately upheld by the stalwart, steadfast character of his own unsupported faith. The saving power of vicarious faith is demonstrated in our homes repeatedly. The Christian home, by definition, is that place to which, over and over again, the husband and father can return defeated and downhearted, at the end of his rope and faith, and there find in the home enough faith and compassion, and tender understanding, for two people! And there is no law against this principle of vicarious faith working in reverse. Parents provide such faith for their children; and frequently, praise God, children all unknowingly return the compliment of faith. The faith that saves at any given moment is exercised by the body of believers. So it has been throughout all ages in the church, the body of believers on earth.

Incidentally, here is found the justification for infant Baptism. Many sincere Christians take the argument I was using a moment ago about the necessity for faith in the valid celebration of the sacraments to argue, " Well, a tiny baby in arms cannot possibly believe, so the sacrament cannot be valid in such a situation." But it is not the baby who is called upon to believe; it is the father and the mother and the believing church. The whole point is here: The child will never come to believe unless somebody starts believing for him and providing an atmosphere of faith, a climate of love, so that, through the promises made and implemented both by the believing parents and the believing church, the child is taught and led to believe for himself. This is the meaning of the Christian home and the Christian church and herein consists the church's program of Christian education.

The body of believers exists to communicate to me in the days when my individual faith is weak, and the flame of my personal love burns low, that sufficiency of strength and courage and hope which will enable me to ride out the storm and believe again myself, in God's own good time. The church does this through the Christian fellowship, the mutually ministered, the corporately celebrated sacraments of grace, evidences of the forgiveness of God, communicated through the tangible tokens of a love that will not let any of us go. So from the beginning of the days when the resurrected Christ walked and talked among his friends in a renewed fellowship of faith and love, " those who received his word were baptized, and . . . devoted themselves to the apostles' teaching and fellowship, to the breaking of bread and the prayers." This is a belief that matters.

A PRIMER FOR PRAYER

"L ORD, teach us to pray." (Luke 11:1.) This is a curious request. For the men who addressed this request to Jesus were all religious men, devout Jews. They had been praying all their lives. That is to say, ever since they could remember they had periodically participated in the prescribed ritual of the Temple. But this was just the difficulty. They had come to believe that access to God was provided only by the set ritual, meticulously administered by skilled and dedicated priests, and that only as the prayers of sinful men were upheld, directed, and implemented by such sacrosanct mediators could they gain indirect entrance into the Holy of Holies, become assured participants in the grace of God. They realized that they did not know how to pray *for* themselves, that this priceless, dangerous freedom was an area in which they had no practical experience.

Why was it that Jesus Christ inveighed so relentlessly against the Pharisees? Because they had sold themselves and a highly religious people on the thesis that sinful man had no way of coming to grips intimately and personally with God in prayer except through the prescribed ritual, the prescribed organization. "You must go through channels." Such was the Pharisaic code. Jesus Christ came into the world to induce in sinful man only one great saving conviction: every individual man, sinner though he may be, still has immediate access to the throne of grace. It was not an accident that when Jesus Christ hung upon his cross " the veil of the temple was rent . . . from the top to the bottom." The symbol which man in his pride and fear had erected as a kind of iron curtain, of necessity keeping man away from God, was revealed at last to be what it had always been, so far as God is concerned — nonexistent.

Why was it that Jesus Christ threw the money-changers out of the Temple? It was not because they were handling money in the Temple, nor because they were doubtless cheating while they were handling money in the Temple. He threw out the " middlemen " who had taken upon themselves to say to earnest seekers after God, " You must convert the coin of the realm, of everyday life, into our special brand of money, with which you may then go to the stalls and buy the sacred ox or the sacred lamb or the sacred dove, and so suitably present yourselves and your offerings before God." Those who thus interjected themselves between man and God were in anger rebuked: " God says, ' My house shall be a house of prayer for *all* people,' and you have made it a den of thieves. You have stolen away man's rights. Sinful man by reason of God's everlasting mercy has immediate access to God without any middleman." This was an entirely new idea to the first followers of Jesus Christ. And so they came to him imploring, "Lord, teach us to pray."

A woman called me one evening, asking me if I would pray for a friend of hers in deep distress, and adding, " Because you know your prayers, as a minister, will be so much more efficacious than mine." I didn't argue with her — she was in no mood for argument. All I said was, " Of course, I will join my prayers with yours for your friend." But how tragically wrong she was! The minister's prayers are no more efficacious at the throne of grace than any other man's. Indeed, in the first instance, every man must learn to pray for himself, "Lord, teach *me* to pray." You don't have to ask anybody else. You don't have to ask a "saint." You don't have to ask the Virgin Mary. You don't have to ask anybody to take you into the presence of the love that will not let you go. *You* must ask for yourself, and *you* will receive. *You* must seek for yourself, and *you* will then find. *You* must knock for yourself, and to *you* it will then be opened. *You must learn to pray!*

The disciples' request seems equally strange for a quite opposite reason. Why *learn* to do something that "comes natural," as the boys say? For prayer is natural; all persons pray at times, in spite of themselves, do they not? One of the most helpful books on prayer I ever read was written many years ago by Harry Emerson Fosdick when he was a very young man. *The Meaning of Prayer* contains a chapter entitled "The Naturalness of Prayer." Prayer *is* natural; so why learn to pray? Carlyle has written, "Prayer remains the native and deepest impulse of the soul of man." Carlyle was right. Epictetus has truly said: "When thou hast shut thy door and darkened thy room, say not to thyself that thou art alone. God is in thy room." All of us have had this experience. Dr. Fosdick cites an instance in the Civil War when a dying soldier, terribly wounded in the terrific battle at Fort Wagner, was being comforted by his chaplain. The chaplain asks, "Son, do you ever pray?" And the boy replies: "Sometimes. I prayed last Saturday night at Wagner. I guess everybody prayed then." Indeed, there is that helpless time and that fearful place when "everybody" prays. Surely no thoughtful man has ever lived long but has experienced the agony that overwhelmed the soul of Abraham Lincoln: "I have been driven many times to my knees by the overwhelming conviction that I had nowhere else to go; my own wisdom and that of all around me seemed insufficient for the day." By reason of our spiritual nature and of our own soul's deepest need, prayer is natural. " Deep calls to deep."

But to do effectively what one does naturally must be learned and taught. Therefore, " Lord, teach us to pray." The baby will inevitably talk, though we have visions of his going away to college without uttering a syllable! But he will learn to talk because he is taught to talk. Man is a gregarious animal; he is designed for fellowship with others of his own kind. But he must be educated to enter into healthy, helpful human relationships — this is the greatest problem of the world. Man does not inevitably do well what he does naturally. Education consists in the training and development of man's natural capacity to walk, to talk, to enter into fellowship. A man can learn to drive a car, he can learn to fly, but he *has to learn*. You can teach a youngster to swim, so it is said, by taking him to the deep end of the dock and pushing him off. People have learned to swim that way, but never well. No one ever qualified for the Olympics that way. Hence, " Lord, teach us to pray."

But in a very real sense, prayer is not natural to sinful man. In making this request, the disciples prove that they have already passed over a great spiritual divide. For " to pray " is the exact antithesis of man's pride. We are caught in a dilemma: we have to pray and we really don't want to pray! Let's face it. It is all very well for Jesus Christ to say, " Ask, and it will be given you," but I don't like to ask! I like to do it for myself or, if somebody's going to do it for me, I prefer it be done without the humiliation I endure in asking for it. When Christ says to me, " Seek and you will find," I don't want to seek — at least not very hard and not very long, and

I don't particularly care to be in the seeker's position. I do not like to confess that I do not know all the answers. My ego resents having to hunt for them, having to ask somebody's help in discovering them and, once they are discovered, in understanding them and, once they are understood, in applying them. " Knock, and it will be opened." But this is inhospitable; it denies my *right* of entrance. I much prefer the " open-door policy." In order to pray, I must become humble and I don't want to be humble. So I must be taught to be humble. Sinful, arrogant, proud, independent man *does not want to pray.*

Pride made Adam the original " fall guy " in the Garden of Eden. The devil said to him: " If you will eat of the fruit of the tree of knowledge, you won't ever have to pray again. You won't ever have to ask God for anything. You'll have it, brother! It will all be yours! " Man does not like to prostrate himself in prayer, yet real prayer permits no other position for the soul. " Blessed are the poor in spirit," Jesus said, " for *theirs* is the kingdom of heaven. . . . Except ye turn and become as a little child, you will in no wise enter into the kingdom of heaven." The disciples had come a long way when they implored, " Lord, teach us to pray."

They did not ask, " Lord, teach us *how* to pray." True, there are mechanics, there are times and seasons, but, believe me, they are relatively unimportant. The abysmal need of the human heart is not *how* to pray, but to *pray.* Lord, give us the spirit of prayer, the willingness to pray. Make us to be *glad* in our dependence upon prayer, in a sense of security deeper than the answers we shall never know, in an assurance above and beyond the requests that will not be granted in this lifetime; in the mystery that will not be rent before our sin-filled eyes, but that we come to trust — through prayer — as a love that will not let us go. In true prayer we make a commitment of self to that which we do not completely understand, and in that commitment we find rest unto our souls. Lord, teach us so to pray.

The prodigal son had never really prayed in his life (true, he had asked for things, but only in order to escape out of the prayer relationship) until that day in the far-off country when he finally came to himself and said: " I will go home, and I will begin to ask my father for those things that hitherto I have been unwilling even to admit to myself I needed to have, or if I ever discerned that I needed them, I was reluctant to seek them except for myself and by myself alone. I will go home and I will say to my father: ' Father, I have sinned against heaven and in thy sight and am no longer worthy to be called thy son. I've stepped out of the prayer relationship long ago. Now make me as one of thy hired servants. Start telling me what it is I ought to do and be! ' "

But that boy had to go back home for himself — nobody could go back for him. He did not need a priest — the priest would simply have gotten in the way. All that a priest or the minister can do for you is to say, " Go home; the door is open." But you must go to God in prayer; no man can go for you. Because we are uncertain of the way, we cry, " Lord, teach us to pray." Here was Jesus' answer: " When you go into your room " — not a priest within a hundred miles, no ecclesiastical trimmings, no spiritual red tape, nothing but you, a sinner, face to face with God. He will not give you all the answers you think you must have right now — even in your prayer closet. You will come out many a day as perplexed as when you walked in. But in time you may come out with the realization that God is there, that he knows you and your need as you do not, and that he asks you to walk

with him in trust even though the balance sheet of the so-
called facts of life doesn't always add up on any given day! //
" Lord, teach us to pray."

We want to pray and we don't want to pray. We have
needs, but we should be happier if we could fill them ourselves. We have questions, and the answers ought to be given
to us far more easily than they are given. We go through
life really filled with a great deal of prejudice and resentment
and even hatred against God Almighty because he refuses
to let us in on everything he is doing for us and through us.
Much of our praying becomes a frantic, fruitless beating upon
the door of heaven to force issues that cannot be forced, to
present " demand notes " not yet due. Rarely do we get down
to where our fundamental, really basic need to pray is: simply
to present ourselves to God as we are, somehow, some way,
sometime, every single day and say: " Take thou my hand,
dear Lord. Lead thou me on," and let it go at that!

What more do we want? What more can we get? The answer to prayer is God himself. At the end of his answer to
the disciples' request, Jesus uses the analogy he so often employed, the parent-child relationship. " You who are all-too-
human fathers, selfish, ignorant, with but partial understanding and limited vision — your children come to you, hungry,
and ask for food. They ask for a fish, or an egg. Ignorant
though you are, selfish though you are, you know enough
and you are kind enough not to give them that which will
not only not help but hurt — you will not give them snakes
or scorpions! Now, believe me, God is at least as good as
you are. If you then, who are evil, know how to give good
gifts to your children, how much more will the Heavenly
Father give you — the Holy Spirit." That is all. But that is
enough. What would you gain through prayer more needful
than the spirit of patience, of humility, of waiting in trust,

of commitment, of reconciliation, of the peace that passes understanding? In answer to prayer Christ promises, "My peace I give to you."

> "Be not afraid to pray, to pray is right.
> Pray, if thou canst with hope, but ever pray,
> Though hope be weak — or sick with long delay.
> Pray in the darkness, if there be no light.
>
> . . . .
>
> Whate'er is good to wish, ask that of heaven,
> Though it be what thou canst not hope to see;
> Pray to be perfect, though material leaven
> Forbid the spirit so on earth to be;
> But if for any wish thou canst not pray,
> Then pray to God to cast that wish away."

("Prayer," by Hartley Coleridge, in *Quotable Poems,* Vol. I, p. 135. Willett, Clark & Company.)

"Lord, teach us so to pray." This is a belief that matters.

THE STEPLADDER OF THE SOUL

THE amazing fact about Jesus' reply to the earnest request of the disciples, "Lord, teach us to pray," is the complete absence of emphasis on mechanics or techniques. Neither by precept nor by example did Jesus Christ leave behind a "handbook" on *how* to pray. We know of course, from his own habits, that he felt the need for regular participation in the experience of group worship. "He went to the synagogue, as his custom was, on the sabbath day." We also know that he did not completely adjust himself to the Temple ritual; he did not always go there when other people thought he ought to. We know he was violently opposed to the prostitution of ritual which prevented it from being what it was meant to be — a means of grace, which kept the Temple from being a "house of prayer for all people." We know that Jesus frequently — but there is no suggestion as to the regularity — went off by himself and spent long periods in personal prayer. But if he had any set way of "saying his prayers," he never passed it on, even to his inner circle of friends.

He did give us what we call "the Lord's Prayer," and I am sure he would not object to our using it as an integral part of group worship. But the Lord's Prayer is not a tech-

nique of how to pray; it is an exposition of the spirit of
prayer. It is a reminder of the necessity of prayer and of what
we ought to pray for. Jesus seemed convinced that when a
man really wanted to pray, he would pray — with varied
technique. The important thing was to get a man to want to
pray, and, more important, to get a man to believe that God
wants him to pray, that there is a love that wants to hear
and to answer real prayer. So in reply to the question, Jesus
made two very simple but fundamental suggestions:

First, " when you pray, go into your room and shut the
door and pray to your Father . . . in secret." (Matt. 6: 6.)
This can be done on the spur of the moment, or it may take
days and weeks to bring the reluctant soul to push through
that door and enter into God. Once " the secret place of the
most High " is entered, the prayer experience may be prolonged or brief. Augustine wrote out of experience, " We
may pray most when we say the least, and we may pray the
least when we say the most! " The problem is to *want* to go
in and really do the business that can properly be transacted
on the other side of that door. It doesn't necessarily take a
long time to pray — it often takes a long time to *want* to
pray. Even after the soul goes in, there can be an hour's
wrestling in doubt and anxiety, or a repeated audience is
sought and given behind shut doors until the " still small
voice " is heard and heeded above the tumult of the world
without and the tempest of the soul within. The time and
the place are immaterial — " prayer " is all-essential. True
prayer is the soul in voluntary and solitary confrontation
with its God — seeking newness of life and light and love.

I remind you that a child can be born at any hour, day or
night, and the travail at birth may be long and the delivery
difficult; or the new life can upon occasion make its appear-
ance with astounding ease and speed, possibly before the

hospital is even reached! A man can drop dead in the twin-
kling of an eye, or he can die by inches and over months of
time. There is no pattern for physical birth or death, and
there are no rigid rules governing either the death of the soul
or the rebirth and restoration of that soul through prayer. A
man is not really praying until he takes the basic issues and
decisions of his life into the conscious presence of God alone,
who made him and who has revealed His will and purpose in Jesus Christ, and there spreads them out — whether
small or great — and invites the divine concern and the
divine control. When he has done that, he has prayed — the
rest is up to God. All Jesus sets as the inviolate rule governing
the growth of the soul is, "When you pray, go into your
room and shut the door and pray to your Father in secret;
and your Father who sees in secret will reward you."

In the second place, when you pray, "use not vain repeti-
tions [the preceding clause is King James Version], as the
Gentiles do; . . . for your Father knows what you need"
(Matt. 6: 7 ff.). This second suggestion of Jesus concerning
prayer is so absolutely contrary to our naturally selfish way
of using all God's good gifts, including the gift of prayer,
that we must ask ourselves, "Well, if this is so, then why
pray at all? " Which simply means we do not know what it
means to *pray*. We think of prayer as a kind of special delivery chute down which God's good gifts — material things
or health — will slide swiftly and directly into our lives,
when actually, at least for Jesus Christ, prayer is the step-
ladder of the soul by which we climb to God, and by which
he descends to us. It is the way by means of which I permit
his Spirit to bring me around to his way of looking at life
and so introduce myself into his will for my life. This does
not destroy the element of " petition " in prayer, but it vastly

changes the nature and relevance of " petition " — it puts it in its proper place.

Petition for physical things is the " kindergarten " stage in the relationship of the soul to God as in the relationship of the child in his home. It constitutes a very proper part of prayer — an inescapable part. The six-weeks-old baby cries and that cry is a prayer, and the loving father and mother immediately rush to answer the prayer. But when that tiny boy is sixteen years old, if he's still crying for the same things, then there's something wrong with the child or with the home in which he has spent sixteen years! His petitions ought to change. Many of them are still for material help, things he can't do by himself. A boy away at college should write home when he needs money, but if he never writes home except when he needs money, there is still something wrong — either with the boy or with the home.

Furthermore, somewhere along the line the child learns to trust his parents' love and judgment and not just to place his confidence in the vehemence of his own petition to produce the desired results. Over and over again we organize as a pressure group in prayer; we " lobby " with the Almighty God; we try to " twist his arm." We are frantic and anxious in our praying because we are not really *praying*. We are *telling* God Almighty what has to happen if he is to prove himself good and if we are to remain convinced of his goodness. But this is not responsible prayer! Often a " No " is a *good* answer to prayer, as every wise and loving parent knows. Many times it is a better answer than the " Yes " which the child frantically implores. Often when not getting the " Yes," the child goes out firmly believing that his father and mother do not love him, never did love him, and surely will never understand him. And yet through this very process the child learns to grow up, to know what it is that he really needs his parents for as long as life shall last. Petition for things is the "kindergarten" level of prayer. Whether granted or not, through "Yes" and "No," we learn what prayer is really for.

A higher level of prayer is the level of thanksgiving. Every father and mother spend a considerable amount of time teaching their young children to say thank you. Such a habit is not induced to make the father and mother feel better. This is not a matter of appeasement; it is essential to the spiritual growth of the child. Moreover, it strengthens the child's faith in the love and care of his parents. In our relationship to God, if we thanked him more, we could trust him more. There is good psychology in the counsel of the old hymn: "Count your many blessings, name them one by one, And it will surprise you what the Lord hath done." It will also give you renewed trust in what the Lord is likely to do. One of life's tragedies is that so many men and women never even get up to this primary grade in their praying. They do not give thanks — they do not even say grace at meals.

I repeat, this is not a matter of appeasement. God will continue to make his sun to shine on the just and the unjust, his rain will fall on the righteous and the unrighteous; the man who forgets to give thanks will have it just as good tomorrow as he did yesterday, or as will the man who did give thanks. This is a matter of spiritual growth. Thanksgiving is for the benefit of the soul that gives thanks. Faith is rooted in thanksgiving — "The Lord *is* good; his mercy is everlasting; and his truth endureth to all generations." "Now thank we all our God"!

The next higher level of prayer is confession and the acceptance of forgiveness. Here again, all concerned parents

teach their children to say, " I'm sorry." And again, the motive is not appeasement. Only the child who learns how to
admit his fault in an atmosphere of love and understanding
can escape the sense of estrangement that sin inescapably
breeds. Sin destroys fellowship. The child who has not discovered his dependence for his spiritual security upon the
understanding, compassion, and forgiveness of his own father and mother will grow up into the kind of self-justifying
adult whose terrible insecurity creates misery for himself and
everybody else around him. The world is far too full of just
such adults who have never learned how to admit their own
mistakes; and so have never learned how to accept forgiveness; and so have never learned how to forgive other people.
They are " hard " — they are hard on themselves and they are
hard on everybody around them. The prayer of confession
and assurance of pardon are essential rungs in the ladder of
the prayer life of the soul.

Again, every father and mother worthy of the name teach
their children to condition their own petitions in the light of
the equally clamant needs of their brothers and sisters. This
is "intercessory prayer." The child who has learned to live
in a family relationship wants nothing for himself at the
expense of his brother. He wants for his brother that which
he hopes to receive for himself. Note that in the Lord's
Prayer intercession is inextricably interwoven in every petition. Every pronoun, save the pronouns that refer to God
himself, is plural — every one! " *Our* Father — give *us* this
day *our* daily bread — forgive *us our* debts as *we* forgive —
lead *us* not into temptation." There isn't an individual petition in the whole prayer.

What is the meaning of " intercession "? Intercession is *not*
getting down on your knees and asking God to do something
for somebody else that won't cost you a dime or a single

ounce of effort. In Luke's account, when Jesus replied to the disciples' request, "Teach us to pray," he told the story of the friend who went to his neighbor at midnight. He said: "I have a friend who has come to me. He's gotten me up in the middle of the night. I find I don't have the resources with which to help him. I am willing to help him, but I can't do it alone. You will have to help me to help him." When the traveler knocked on that door in the middle of the night, the man within didn't say, "Go across the street and ask Brother Jones if he won't put you up." He took him in, and then found that he couldn't do it alone, and *he* went to Brother Jones. This is intercessory prayer. This may not be the only kind of intercessory prayer there is — but it is the only kind Jesus talked about. When you pray, say, "Our Father," and begin to act accordingly. "If any one has the world's goods and sees his brother in need, yet closes his heart against him, how does God's love abide in him?" (I John 3: 17.)

The highest level of all prayer is the level of "communion." Here again, the analogy of the family relationship seems to ring true. How every parent longs for the day when the maturing child voluntarily seeks companionship with his parents for the sake of companionship alone — when the child enters into the ideals and hopes and prayers of his father and mother out of no compulsion save that he wants to do it! How heart-warming the phrase in a letter from a college student away from home saying, "I'll never get beyond wanting to put out my hand like a little child in every experience of joy or disappointment." The line of the familiar hymn breathes the spirit of communion in prayer: "Through cloud and sunshine, O abide with me." If you love, you want your sorrow halved and your joy doubled through participation in each and every experience with the beloved.

All this is prayer. Whatever else we learn in life, we must

learn to pray. It is not a matter of form or of mechanics, but of spirit and of truth. And we must learn to pray as spiritual adults. We shall never grow beyond the need of petition, and we need never be afraid to ask God for *anything*. But too many grownups still pray as children, frantically, fearfully, faithlessly — in order to test what they should trust. In prayer as in no other area of life it is essential that we put into practice the exhortation of Paul: " When I was a child, I spoke like a child, I thought like a child, I reasoned like a child; when I became a man, I gave up childish ways " (I Cor. 13: 11).

When *you* pray, " do not heap up empty phrases as the Gentiles do . . . , for your Father knows what you need before you ask him. . . . Seek first his kingdom [the kingdom of commitment in trust] . . . and all these things shall be yours as well." This is a belief that matters.

THE DIVINE COMPANION

As we have seen, Jesus' promise to the disciples' plea, "Lord, teach us to pray," concluded with the rich assurance that the Father will "give the Holy Spirit to those who ask him." In John's Gospel, Jesus is recorded as having promised to make this priceless gift the subject of his own petition to God: "And I will pray the Father, and he shall give you another Comforter, that he may abide with you for ever" (John 14: 16).

The word translated "Comforter" in the King James Version (and less helpfully and no more accurately — as I think — rendered "Counselor" in the Revised Standard Version) is "Paraclete" — literally, "the-one-called-beside." Our most understandable synonym today is probably "Companion." The Holy Spirit is the divine Companion along life's pilgrim way.

The conscious possession of the Holy Spirit is thus the end result of "saving faith." What is the gospel — the good news? Just this: God, from whom man is separated by his own pride and fear, has provided a way and offers a grace whereby man who is desperately alone in his Sin can enter into a renewed fellowship with God. The gift of the Holy Spirit is the sign and seal of that restored relationship. Indeed, it is that relationship restored in man's conscious and grateful acceptance; it is the continuation, for every believing soul and for a believing church in all ages, of that reality of forgiveness which once in history clothed itself in Jesus Christ, " the Word . . . made flesh," and once upon this earth was " Emmanuel " — " God with us." The Holy Spirit is " the Comforter " precisely because he is " the-one-called-beside " us; he is " God-with-us."

It is all very well for Robert Browning to sing with Pippa, " God's in his heaven — all's right with the world! " But anyone past the age of Pippa knows that all is not right with himself or his world. The world of the human heart and the world about it are alike filled with guilt and despair. I can never walk alone through this " vale of tears " sustained only by the knowledge of an " absentee God." I need a road companion; I need a sovereign love that will leave its high throne and walk with me in dark places of my life. Then with David, I might sing, " Yea, though I walk through the valley of the shadow of death, I will fear no evil: for *thou* art *with me*."

The captain of a U. S. Navy destroyer with almost empty fuel tanks, tossed about like a cork in a raging Pacific typhoon during World War II, was little comforted by the thought of the admiral of the fleet safe berthed in the Hawaiian Islands. " Nimitz is in Honolulu — all's right with the fleet! " He was comforted by the captain of a tanker who, sharing the peril, swung his ship alongside and at a tremendous risk pumped fuel oil into the destroyer's tanks, thus providing both ballast and motive power! So to my beleaguered soul the Comforter brings proof that " warm, sweet, tender, even yet A present help is He; And faith has still its Olivet, And love its Galilee " (John G. Whittier).

The Holy Spirit is God's answer to man's deepest hunger — a hunger for a conscious personal relationship with God.

For although sinful man in his pride has severed diplomatic relations with God, he still cannot change his God-given nature. He still cannot escape from being that creature with an affinity for God. So there is an essential loneliness of the human soul which only God can fill. No one has ever expressed it better than Augustine: "Thou has made us for thyself, and our hearts are restless until they find their rest in thee."

The tragedy of our sinful state is that, having "disaffiliated" from God, we frantically seek to fill the aching void perpetually within us with things which can never fill it. We try to dump in "things" — material values and material securities — and we still live with a bottomless pit at the center of our lives. We try to fill it with "hard work" — the hardest kind of work in behalf of the most excellent causes — and still we are "empty." We try pouring into the spiritual abyss irrational amounts of "pleasure" — liquor, the delights of the flesh — still we hunger and thirst.

Most serious of all, we try to squeeze out of a human relationship that which no human relationship can provide — the perfect love and understanding and forgiveness of God. We warp and distort and "break" the affections of those closest to us by trying to make our loved ones serve a need in us that only God can fill. That which we call "possessive love" has this aching void inadequately filled as its source and center. Samuel H. Miller analyzes the danger: "This is our peril, that we may try to satisfy our loneliness for God with the affection of men. . . . Social relationships, however just and morally good, cannot take the place of a spiritual relationship with God. The sum of all creatures will not assuage the thirst of man for the Creator. We may run out the tender, fragile strands of human fellowship in a thousand directions but the resultant cobweb of mere gregariousness will not hide the yawning depths of that deeper hunger." (*The Life of the Soul,* pp. 59–60; Harper & Brothers, 1951. Used by permission.)

Husbands and wives, parents and children, demand from each other a perfection of performance, a depth of understanding, that the human being needs but can never give. Then we are tempted to blame a finite human relationship for failing to provide the love of God. We blame it for revealing itself to be what it inescapably is — an imperfect relationship incapable of ministering to our deepest need — the need for God. And still our poverty of spirit cries out for the riches of God's grace. " My heart and my flesh crieth out for the living God! " To this cry Jesus Christ gave answer: " Blessed are the poor in spirit: for theirs is the kingdom of heaven. Blessed are they that mourn: for they shall be comforted. . . . Blessed are they which do hunger and thirst after righteousness: for they shall be filled. . . . And I will pray the Father, and he shall give you another Comforter, that he may abide with you for ever."

The comfort that the Holy Spirit, the divine Companion, brings is forgiveness accepted for past sin, strength felt for present inadequacy, and hope experienced for future perfection.

There is nothing you and I need so much as we need to accept forgiveness for the past. Dr. Miller's insight again yields the incisive word about the gift of forgiveness: " Nothing keeps us running so madly from one thing to another as our guilt. We did not do the last thing very well so now we will try to do this a little better. And this does not get done either, so we drive ourselves from thing to thing, never accomplishing quite what we wanted to, and accumulating guilt all the while beneath us and in back of us that presses us still on and on with increasing terror and haunting power.

God says: 'Forget it; I have forgiven you; let it go, be quiet, be still, and know that I am God.' With all your fretful anxieties you cannot bring the Kingdom of God. I have made it; I have brought it into being; I have created it; and here it is in men's hearts waiting. You did not put it there and you did not make it by your actions. All that you can do is to see it and to love it and to affirm it and to accept it. It is yours for nothing; you are forgiven. I have made the sun to rise upon the good and on the evil, and you are evil as well as good. I have made the rain to fall upon the just and the unjust. And this magnificence of mercy, of which there is no limit, comes upon us to give us freedom, the freedom of faith in God, that God does care for us and that in his providence there is a peace that the world can neither give nor take away." (*Op. cit.,* pp. 108–109.)

But we not only need forgiveness for the past; we need strength in present weakness. Paul came to a point in his own life where he felt sure that he could not go on burdened with a sense of complete inadequacy. Then the word came to him: " My grace is sufficient for you, for my power is made perfect in [your] weakness." Paul *did* go on — still weak, still knowing he was weak, still feeling weak, still not understanding how on earth he was going to do it! You and I are tempted to place far too great a premium on *how we feel.* God does not promise us we will always *feel* strong. The promise is that we shall have the strength to go on even when we feel we do not have it. A verse from one of our finest hymns paraphrases the promise of the divine Companion, the Comforter:

> "Fear not, I am with thee, O be not dismayed;
> For I am thy God, and will still give thee aid;
> I'll strengthen thee, help thee, and cause thee to stand,
> Upheld by my righteous, omnipotent hand."

The promise of the Holy Spirit is that he will dwell with us and be in us, regardless of how we feel! He does not come and go in accordance with the way we feel. My feelings must not become the test of God's faithfulness.

One of the great glories of our human life is the demonstrated evidence of the presence of the Comforter in the lives of imperfect, faltering, failing men and women who " out of weakness were made strong." I have seen ordinary folk like you and me conduct themselves as valiant warriors in an unremitting struggle, often cast down, but ever rising again; I have seen burdens heavy to be borne, yet borne with high courage and dauntless faith; I have witnessed fierce temptations fought and fought again, often with a broken sword and a battered shield, many an encounter lost, but many an onslaught stemmed and stayed and the field never quitted; I have beheld sorrows and sufferings like a swollen tide and a mighty current threatening to sweep away every anchorage and security of the human spirit stood up to and breasted and souls grown strong in the doing! And I am not alone in witnessing such miracles. Look about you! You can see them every day in the lives of men and women like yourselves. For to us all the promise is given: " My power is made perfect in [your] weakness."

Yet one more gift the Comforter must bring to us, the priceless gift of hope — the hope of future perfection. For every man does hunger and thirst after righteousness; every man made in the image of God and born for fellowship with the spirit of God longs to be filled! Every man wants passionately to be better than he now is; every man wants to be as good as he can be!

But this " righteousness " is ever beyond us. It is something we cannot bring to birth of ourselves. It is born of a union with God himself; it is conceived by the Holy Spirit.

We acquire righteousness as we acquire all spiritual values, not by intellectual struggle, not even by ethical or moral striving. We come to possess righteousness by a kind of spiritual osmosis in close companionship with Him who alone is righteous.

And this takes time — more time than we are allotted on earth. We shall never be satisfied with less than our best — perfection of heart and hand. We were made, we dimly sense, for such perfection. Our twofold task is to accept our present imperfection as God accepts it in forgiveness, even while we continue to believe in that which alone will ultimately satisfy our need and God's desire, " the fulness of the stature of Christ." This is perforce a long, slow, tortuous process. Our fathers called it " sanctification."

Another name for the Holy Spirit is " Sanctifier." The process involved is not always comfortable — but it is comforting! The knowledge that the goal of his painful tutelage is the perfection we wistfully seek is the most comforting thought in the world. Such spiritual growth involves a repeated dying of " the old man," with his affections and lusts, and the repeated birth of a " new man," so that the Christian life becomes a series of reiterated resurrections.

This characteristic of the life of the soul reminds us that many texts in the New Testament that have become largely relegated for use at funerals alone are really meant to be applied to daily life. Take the verse in Revelation where John hears the voice from heaven promising, " Behold, I make all things new. . . . Write: for these words are true and faithful " (Rev. 21:5). Dr. Miller helpfully comments: " You will know a thousand deaths before you die. Your soul will grow slack and weary and will lie down and die. It will be as if it were buried, many times. And then, out of newness of life you shall find a resurrection and in that resurrection all things shall be made new and you will enter into a larger abundance than ever before. But it will only be if you have the strength to confess you have died and want to be resurrected and will enter through travail into a greater glory and a wider abundance and a deeper eternity. 'We must find some place,' said Yeats, 'upon the Tree of Life for the phoenix nest.'" (*Op. cit.,* pp. 119–120.)

Comforted in hope by the presence of the divine Companion, we can cry with the psalmist: "Why art thou cast down, O my soul? And why art thou disquieted within me? Hope thou in God: for I shall yet praise him, who is the health of my countenance, and my God." By the power of the Holy Spirit the soul is a phoenix which will rise again and yet again from the ashes of defeat and despair into the growing likeness of the Son of God. "For we experience not now what we shall be, but we know that when he shall appear, we shall be like him." (I John 3: 2.)

The gospel of Jesus Christ is the good news: "We are not alone" in guilt, in inadequacy, in hopelessness. If we feel so, it is never because God has failed to fulfill the prayer of Christ and his own promise, but rather because we have failed to receive in faith the Comforter.

> "Our blest Redeemer, ere he breathed
> His tender last farewell,
> A Guide, a Comforter, bequeathed
> With us to dwell."

The prerequisite to this priceless gift is never our merit, only our need. Jesus Christ has promised this need will be filled: "And I will pray the Father, and he shall give you another Comforter, that he may abide with you for ever; even the Spirit of truth." As David Livingstone observed, "It is the promise of a gentleman of the strictest honor."

In this promise is fufilled the whole purpose of God in the creation of man, his child: " And the Lord God formed man of the dust of the ground, and breathed into his nostrils the breath of life; and man became a living soul." Defiled, dejected, and defeated, our souls now claim the life-restoring promise of our Lord and Savior: " And . . . he breathed on them, and said to them, ' Receive the Holy Spirit.' " This is *the* belief that matters.